SAINTS AND THEIR STORIES

SAINTS AND THEIR STORIES

by
Peggy Webling

Illustrated by
Frederick Cayley Robinson

THE CENACLE PRESS
AT SILVERSTREAM PRIORY

© 2025 Silverstream Priory

Originally published in 1919 by Nisbet & Co. Ltd of London.

This revised edition, published by
the Cenacle Press at Silverstream Priory,
incorporates some minor alterations to the text.

All reservable rights reserved.

The Cenacle Press at Silverstream Priory
Silverstream Priory
Stamullen, County Meath, K32 T189, Ireland
www.cenaclepress.com

ISBN 978-1-915544-55-1

Book design by Kenneth Lieblich
Cover design by Silverstream Priory

CONTENTS

Saint Christopher	1
Saint Denis	15
Saint Helena	23
Saint Alban	31
Saint George	43
Saint Nicholas	55
Saint Ambrose	67
Saint Martin of Tours	77
Saint Augustine of Hippo	91
Saint Bride	103
Saint Gregory the Great	113
Saint Augustine of Canterbury	123
Saint Etheldreda	133
Saint Swithin	145
Saint Dunstan	155
Saint Hugh of Lincoln	171
Saint Zita	195
Saint Francis of Assisi	207
Saint Catherine of Siena	227
Saint Joan of Arc	239

ILLUSTRATIONS

Saint Christopher	viii
Saint Helena	22
Saint George	42
Saint Martin of Tours	76
Saint Bride	102
Saint Etheldreda	132
Saint Dunstan	154
Saint Hugh of Lincoln	170

ST CHRISTOPHER

SAINT CHRISTOPHER

Third Century
Festival ✦ July 25th

Whoso looks upon the face of Christopher shall not on that day die any evil death. — Old motto

THIS is the story of St Christopher. He was a great soldier who fought under the banner of many kings, and his mighty deeds are told in a collection of famous poems, called *The Golden Legend,* written over seven hundred years ago.

There are only two actual facts known about Christopher. The first, that he was baptised a Christian by a bishop named Babylus of Antioch; the second, that he was martyred for his faith in the third century after the death of our Lord.

These are the actual facts, but the grand old legend that we should read and tell one another at the summer festival held in his honour in July gives us the story of his warrior life.

Christopher was not our saint's original name. Some say that he was called Reprobus, meaning 'the worthless one'; others that his name was Offero, or 'the bearer'.

He was a giant in strength, 'of a right good stature', we read in *The Golden Legend,* 'and he had a terrible and fearful cheer and countenance'.

It is not strange that he should have made up his mind, when a boy, to become a fighter, but he thought little at that time of the different causes for which men fight. He only wished to prove his own strength and serve the most powerful leader, whom he might follow from victory to victory.

At first he enlisted in the bodyguard of a famous emperor of Greece – for Offero lived in a country ruled by the Greeks – and he very soon became the champion of the army. But in a few years, when his emperor was conquered, Offero offered his sword to the victor, so great a king that Offero thought he was the greatest in the world and rejoiced to become his soldier.

'My king is without fear', he said; 'I will follow him to the death'.

Offero was wrong. It is true his king was afraid of no living man, but he dared not face the Prince of Evil. Indeed, he was always thinking of the Prince of Evil. Offero saw how frequently he made the Sign of the Cross and was very puzzled over it.

He did not hesitate to question the king.

'Why dost thou touch thy forehead and thy breast in the form of a cross, my lord?' he asked in his bold, blunt way.

'Because it is the holy sign to drive the devil from me', answered the king.

'Then dost thou fear this devil?' cried Offero in surprise.

'I fear that he will seize upon my soul'.

And again the king made the Sign of the Cross.

The giant Offero said no more, but that night, when the king and his officers were sleeping, he rose from the ground, softly girded on his long sword, and stole away from his comrades.

'Farewell!' he murmured, giving one glance towards the spot where his lord was lying; 'I go to find the great king thou fearest. I will serve that devil who would dare to snatch thy soul. He must be the bravest warrior in the world'.

So he strode out into the night seeking for the Prince of Evil.

On the following day, when the sun was high in the heavens, Offero found himself in the depths of a great forest. It was almost black with the branches of the trees interlaced overhead, and the earth was sodden and cold underfoot.

Suddenly he saw a troop of horsemen riding towards him. They looked like shadows, silent and sombre. Their leader was clad in black armour, and black plumes waved from his helmet.

He drew rein when he saw the great form of Offero standing in his path, questioned him, and, stooping forward in his saddle, gazed at him long and sternly with his deep-set, sullen eyes. His face was terrible to look upon, but the young soldier was not afraid.

He boldly told his story.

'I am the king thou seekest', said the black rider; 'I am the leader of the powers of evil. Wilt thou dare to follow me?'

Offero laughed with wild delight. He had met the greatest king in the world! He seized the bridle of the black rider's black horse.

'I will fight for thee. I will die in thy service. I am thine till I find a greater lord!'

So the shadowy troop rode on, with the devil and his new soldier at its head.

Insolent pride and arrogance filled the heart of Offero. He rejoiced in the fearful power of the black rider, served him in folly and blindness, and obeyed his most ruthless commands.

Wherever the Prince of Evil led, he followed. They rode through the open country by night, killing and plundering, and revelled in the dense forest by day. At first Fury, and then Despair, two of the most harsh and merciless of the black rider's army, became Offero's nearest friends. They never left him. He tried in vain to shake them off, but they were too strong even for his giant strength to master. But still his pride was overweening. He believed his leader to be the greatest king in the world.

One day, as they were hastening towards the forest in the early morning after a night of cruelty and bloodshed, Offero was amazed to see the black rider suddenly stop in his headlong gallop. He dragged his big horse back upon its haunches. He shuddered from head to foot. An expression of abject fear swept over his haughty face, leaving it white and drawn and wrinkled like the skin of a snake.

Then Offero saw at the edge of the road a tall, roughly-hewn wooden cross. The breaking light of dawn touched the figure that hung upon it with soft, pearly colour.

'Why do we stop?' cried the giant soldier. 'Why does my lord tremble? What is there to fear in yonder pale, silent figure of wood?'

The black rider, on the black horse, looked as if he had been turned to marble. He dared not pass the crucifix. So they stood for a long time, Offero in great wonder gazing from one to another, while the powers of evil were cowering and conquered behind their lord.

Then the black rider turned his horse and brutally spurred it forward. There was confusion in all the troop. Horses plunged, a wild cry of panic rushed from a hundred throats, the road was beaten with iron hoofs, and the whole army of the Prince of Evil fled in a cloud of choking dust.

Fury and Despair, once the chosen comrades of Offero, had left him for ever. He was alone beside the cross.

The faint light of dawn deepened and changed until the divine figure on the cross was flooded with rosy light.

The giant soldier folded his hands upon the hilt of his sword and looked at the crucifix. A strange yearning and loneliness possessed him. All the pride of his heart melted away. He knew that he had met at last with the greatest power in the world, but he knew not how to serve his new Lord. Bitter tears crept into his eyes, for he felt as helpless as a weak child, for all his mighty strength of muscle and limb.

He did not understand the meaning of the cross. He only knew that the black rider, whom he had honoured as a king of great kings, had fled in terror before it.

Sadly, slowly, when the long day was over, Offero started out once more to seek his Master – the Man who died upon the cross.

He travelled far, far away, but he could not find Him. He grew very weary, but hope and courage never failed him. From none could he hear where to find the unknown King, though he sought for knowledge from great soldiers, rich and powerful judges, learnèd doctors, wealthy princes and rulers.

At last in a quiet, darkling cave, far from the noise of cities, Offero met with a holy man, old and wise and very humble, who knew of the Lord he longed to serve, and pitied the giant soldier.

As Offero listened to the voice of the hermit, telling him of the life and death of Jesus Christ, his soul was filled with love and longing, and his great heart overflowed. He cast away his sword and knelt at the feet of the holy man.

'Teach me how to serve my King!' he pleaded of him.

'Thou must pray for mercy day and night, my son', said the good hermit.

'Alas! I cannot pray; no words of beauty are known to me', said the rough soldier.

'Thou must fast for many hours', said the holy hermit.

'Alas! I cannot fast', said the rough soldier.

'Thou must turn all thy thoughts to silent adoration of thy King', said the holy hermit.

'Woe is me! I can only fight and work', said the rough soldier.

Offero wept. He wept at the recollection of his wicked life with the powers of evil. He wept the healing tears of repentance. Then the hermit pondered for long, while Offero waited in troubled silence.

'I know of a strong river', said the hermit, 'where many travellers have lost their lives, for no boat can live in its turbulent waters. If thou canst work, it shall be thy task to carry them across the flood. Hast thou the patience to do only this, awaiting the orders of thy King?'

Offero rose from his knees and strode to the mouth of the cave.

'Take me to the river!' he cried.

So the holy hermit took him to the strong river, gave him his blessing, and went away.

Then Offero built him a rough hut of stones and the branches of trees, cut a mighty staff on which to lean his weight when he crossed the flood, and waited for the coming of travellers.

Many of his fellow-men he carried across the river. Many a weary soul would have perished without his help.

Month after month, year after year, in summer heat and winter frost he laboured in sweet content. He dreamed of the Lord he was unable to serve with beautiful words, ever thinking of his own unworthiness.

One night, when the cold winds were howling round his lonely hut, Offero laid him down to sleep. No traveller, he knew, would seek his help to ford the river in a threatened storm.

He heard the beat of rain and rising tide.

As he was sinking into sleep there was the sound

of a voice at the door.

'Offero! Arise and bear Me over the river!'

The strong man sprang up. He opened his door, curious to see the traveller who dared to cross on such a stormy night.

He peered into the thickening darkness, but there was no one to be seen.

'I must have fallen into a dream', he thought, and once more shut out the wind and rain before he stretched himself upon the ground to go to sleep again.

'Offero! Arise and bear Me over the river!'

The voice was louder and more insistent. The words rang out, like a deep bell, through the lashing rain and howling blast.

Offero stood long at his door wondering. He was all alone. The sky was heavy with black clouds. He heard the rushing river and the dull murmur of thunder in the far distance.

For the second time, amazed and strangely moved by the echo in his heart of the ringing voice, he went into his hut and closed his door. He did not lie down to sleep this time, but waited – waited – waited.

'Offero! Arise and bear Me over the river!'

The clear bell had changed into a soft, appealing note of music.

Then Offero leapt out into the night, and he saw,

standing on the river bank below him, the figure of a Child.

Offero's wonder changed to doubt. He knew so well the dangers of the river at flood. But three times the Child had called upon him. The Child was waiting for him now. So he lifted the Boy upon his shoulders, grasped his tall staff in his right hand, and slowly, cautiously, boldly, stepped down into the waters.

They were quickly eddying round his knees. He felt the stones slipping under his feet. The storm clouds burst over his head in torrents of blinding rain.

The weight of the Child was much greater than he had expected. His broad shoulders ached and drooped, but he pressed forward, every muscle taut, every nerve strained.

Soon the waters were swirling as high as his waist, breaking against his chest, splashing his face, gurgling in his ears, rushing through his hair.

His back was bent beneath the mighty weight that he bore upon his shoulders. His huge staff bent under his hand like a reed. Giant trees were uprooted on the river banks, and fell writhing and crashing to earth. The skies were emptied of rain, but lightning flashed unceasingly and thunder roared over his head.

Onward and onward he struggled, breathing hard, now and again shaking the water from his face, with never a word on his lips, never a thought in his soul

– of fear or abandonment of labour.

At last he reached the opposite bank. At last the eddies and the tumbling waves were behind him. At last, at last his task was over!

The Child slipped from his shoulders. Offero drew himself to his full height with a long, deep sigh of gratitude.

'God be praised!' he panted; 'it seemed to me as if I were carrying the weight of the whole world!'

'It is true!' said the Child; 'for thou hast carried Him who carries the sins of the whole world upon thy shoulders tonight'.

A great fear and a great joy seized upon Offero. He knew it was the Holy Child before him. He saw his King in a halo of celestial light.

'Henceforth thou shalt be called Christopher, the Christ-bearer', said the sweet, thrilling voice that stilled the tempest. 'Return to thy hut and thrust thy staff into the earth before thou sleepest'.

And Christopher fell at His feet and worshipped Him.

Then he rose and went back through the now quiet river, obeyed the command of the King by thrusting his staff into the ground outside his door, and, falling down in utter weariness, fell into deep slumber.

The sun was high in the heavens when Christopher awoke, and there were shadows he had never seen before waving and flickering on the walls of his hut.

He went to the door. He threw it open. The rough staff that he had thrust into the earth had grown in the night to a mighty tree, bearing flowers and leaves and fruit. And Christopher knew that it was a sign of the truth of his holy vision.

For many long years St Christopher lived on by the river. His great strength never waned, but he was so gentle and mild, so devout and humble, that the poorest traveller, or the most timid child, was not afraid to ask his help. It is said that ever afterwards, to prove the truth of his name, the Christ-bearer, whenever he stuck his staff into the earth it burst into leaf and blossom.

It is also said that when he left the little hut, his home for so long, it was to journey to a distant land to cheer some unhappy Christians, ill-used by a cruel emperor. He lived among them, loved and loving, until the wicked emperor's wrath was turned against him and he was torn from his poor friends. The emperor's soldiers were amazed at the strength and height of the old man; they listened to his holy words and marvelled at his faith and courage.

The story says that he converted his fierce captors, but their master, the ruthless emperor, would not listen to the words of truth. St Christopher was mocked, tortured, and suffered a cruel martyrdom, but he died as he had lived, faithful to the King of kings, the Holy Child whose power had upheld him in the stormy waters of the darkest night.

So ends the legend of St Christopher.

Do you understand its inner meaning? Can you find the nugget of gold in the dark earth?

The rough soldier Offero found the greatest King in the world when he sought for knowledge from a simple, poor man – the gentle hermit – and he was content to serve that King in humble labour without reward.

The raging river is meant to be the river of life. It was the growing strength of his faith and goodness that upheld the travellers who crossed it. He lessened the weight of the sorrows of the world by lifting his own share as lightly as if it were a little child upon his shoulders. The darkness and storm of night were like the darkness and storm in his own soul when he served the Prince of Evil. It was only when he loved and feared God that he was able to see the bright vision of his Lord.

Let us honour the memory of the great St Christopher.

SAINT DENIS

Third Century
Festival ⚜ October 9th

We build not temples unto our martyrs as unto gods, but memorials unto dead men, whose spirits with God are still living. — St Augustine

THERE are many quaint old pictures of a certain saint, that you are sure to come across some day, which will surprise you very much.

You will see by his robes that he was a bishop. In some of the pictures he holds a sword. He is often painted standing between his two best friends. The strange thing about him is this – he is represented as carrying his head in his hands.

The name of this bishop is Denis, and he is known as the patron saint of France.

Why is it, do you imagine, that the artists of long ago painted St Denis with his head grasped between his own fingers instead of in its right place on his shoulders? The principal reason was to make people remember his brave death, for he was a martyr. That means, he was not afraid to die for the sake of our Saviour, who died for him and all men.

Although St Denis is beloved and honoured more in France than in any other country, he was not a Frenchman.

Born in Italy hundreds of years ago, I cannot tell you anything about his childhood, except that he must have been rather more serious and thoughtful than some boys we know of, for when he was very young the pope sent him to Gaul to tell the people of that country about the Christian religion. He was called a missionary, and accompanied by a few other young men – some people say there were only seven of them altogether, and they knew very little of the strange world beyond Italy.

You must remember it was very difficult and dangerous to travel in those days. Denis and his companions crossed the sea in a small sailing boat. They knew that the land of Gaul was ruled by a very powerful emperor who did not believe in their faith. They knew that the people were bound, partly by fear and partly by old custom, to serve and obey their own priests, who had taught them to worship false gods.

They knew that the life before them would be as rugged as a mountain pass, so hard and wearisome to climb, with its hollow chasms, cruel rocks, perilous, dizzy heights; but it was a life that would lead to the glorious sunshine and pure snows that only the brave and devoted can ever reach.

Of all the companions of St Denis, on that eventful voyage to an unknown land, there were two whom he loved, and who loved him, even more deeply than all the others. These were his friends, a priest called Rusticus and a deacon with the long, rather difficult name of Eleutherius.

Perhaps these two had been companions of St Denis in his boyhood; perhaps they had been schoolfellows; his enthusiasm may have induced them to become missionaries; at all events, nothing is known of the beginning of the friendship, but it is certain that their loyalty never failed him, and you will see, at the end of the story, how they shared in his martyrdom and his triumph.

St Denis and his adventurous companions reached the shores of Gaul in safety. They landed at once, and, very likely before the sun set on the first day, the Apostle of France had spoken the Blessèd Name of Jesus Christ under the open skies. St Denis is called the *Apostle of France,* for Gaul, as you know, was the old name of that lovely land of faith and freedom.

The seven missionaries from Italy made their way to that part of the country where the great city of Paris now stands. They settled on an island in the River Seine.

St Denis must have been a man of great energy,

for it was not long before a church was built where he and his brothers preached, holding regular Masses and striving to win the people to a knowledge of the truth. Their efforts were rewarded, by the blessing of God, with many followers, and they were upheld in all hardship and distress by the living fire of their great faith.

It is hard for you and me to realise the lives of such men as St Denis, his great friends Rusticus and Eleutherius, and their companions.

They were alone in a strange country, among a rough people who could not understand their ideals or rise to their enthusiasm; they had to build their own churches – but that was very fortunate, you know, for only the men who love to build a church can do it well – and they were never free from the dread of persecution.

In other words, the heathen priests of Gaul, supported by the ruler, seized every opportunity to oppose the little band of courageous Christians with falsehood and injustice.

Not that St Denis would have been at all daunted by the most cruel threats. He was one of the early soldiers of the noble army of martyrs, knowing that the post of danger is the place of honour in war.

Many, many years he laboured. Slowly, but surely, as the light of morning spreads over the sky and earth, the Light of the World spread over the land of Gaul.

SAINT DENIS

St Denis was the first Bishop of Paris. We do not know how soon it was before his little band of missionaries was doubled, trebled, multiplied a hundredfold, but there can be no doubt that their example of holiness and devotion was followed by other noble-minded men, and their leader gained in power and right authority.

The distrust of the ruler of the country, added to the jealousy of the pagan priests, became more and more bitter. The people were very ignorant and easily moved to hatred of the strangers – the strangers who had lived so peaceably among them for so long, preaching the mercy of God and the love of Christ.

St Denis was seized at last and thrown into prison. His two most devoted followers, the single-hearted Rusticus and Eleutherius, shared his fate. We do not know whether the three were allowed to be together, but we can be sure that in their thoughts and prayers they were never parted.

The most cruel torture – blind and useless, as all cruelty is – could not break the spirit of the dauntless Denis. I am sure you will think it was very wonderful how an old man, worn and weary with long, long years of toil, could endure such agony. He even rejoiced in it! You see, his whole life had been different from the lives of other men.

His prayers, his thoughts, his deeds, all his hopes

were inspired by the light of God. His heart was filled with aspiration. That is a beautiful word – aspiration. It means a desire for the highest, so strong a love of what is right that every selfish or unkind thought passes away. Suffering for his Lord was welcome to the dying soldier. As I told you before – the greater danger the greater honour, the greater fight the greater victory.

We are told that he was cast among wild beasts, but they refused to harm him and crouched at his feet. Another story is of a great fire that was lighted round a stake to which his heartless enemies had bound him, but the very flames grew cold as they drew near to the holy man.

At last he was beheaded, his beloved Rusticus and Eleutherius dying at the same time.

There is one legend, that the body of St Denis uprose, lifted and carried its own head to the spot where the abbey dedicated to his memory was built in after years, while a choir of angels, singing *Alleluia*, led the way. There is another, that the bodies of the three martyrs were thrown into the River Seine, but a gracious Christian lady of France, named Catulla, rescued and buried them, raising a simple little shrine over the three graves.

Now, it is very possible that the pagan priests and unjust judges who condemned these pure-hearted and heroic men to death thought, in their fools' pride, that

SAINT DENIS

they would be forgotten.

How little they understood the inspiration of St Denis! How little they suspected that the simple shrine, raised by reverent affection and faith by one pious woman, would be changed, after long years, into one of the greatest and most beautiful of French cathedrals, and that the spot on which it stood would be known to all the world by the name of the martyred saint. How little they dreamed that a famous king, Dagobert, would found a monastery there, where the monarchs of France would be laid to rest for generations. How little they knew that the war-cry of their great country would be *Montjoie! St Denis!* Till that time the Gauls had used as their battle-cry the name of the pagan god Jove, but their king, Clovis, who became a Christian, said, 'My Jove shall be St Denis!'

How little, I say, the enemies of the Apostle of France knew that his name would be honoured – honoured and beloved – for centuries!

So, when you see an old picture of a bishop carrying his head in his hands, with a friend on either side, you will know who it is – St Denis of France and his two faithful followers, faithful unto death.

ST HELENA

SAINT HELENA

Fourth Century
Festival ⟶ August 18th

A message from the Heavens whispering to me even in sleep,
These sped me on ... Thou, O God, my life hast lighted.
— Walt Whitman

THIS is the life of a great empress. No book of the legends of the saints should be written without a chapter on the noble, the devout, the radiant Helena.

She was noble in deed, she was devout in thought, she was radiant in beauty, for that word means the brightness of the sun's rays, shining to look upon, like a fine diamond; or better still, the pure dewdrop that glistens on the petals of a flower.

She is a grand and splendid figure in our stories of the saints, this Roman empress, with her gifts, her wealth, her power. Poverty, so beloved by many of the first Christians, did not touch her. She was honoured, admired, and served by men and women who were proud to obey her commands. But at the heart of this great lady, unspoilt by praise or flattery, was the most tender, meek, holy love of our Divine Lord.

Among all the famous people of her time – and it was a very wonderful time in the history of the world – St Helena stands out in her perfect faith. It never wavered from the happy, happy day when the truth burst upon her, lifting her soul to starry heights.

Coël was the name of a king in early Britain. He ruled in that part of the country that is now the county of Essex. The good town of Colchester is supposed to have been called after him.

King Coël had a lovely daughter, and it is believed by a great many people that it was she who became the Empress Helena. Other people say that our saint lived at a tavern and was not a princess at all.

One thing is certain, however, that Helena won the heart of a Roman general, and left our island after marrying him.

The general had a fine Roman name, Constantius Chlorus. He journeyed to Britain with his soldiers, met the lovely maiden, won the consent of her father – and it does not much matter now whether he was a king or a tavern-keeper – and carried her away with him.

She was not a Christian at that time, nor did it seem very likely that Constantius would become an emperor, as he afterwards did. But before that he was made governor of Britain, France, and Spain.

Little is known of St Helena's early married life. Our

English poet, Edmund Spenser, thus describes her in a verse of his poem, *The Faerie Queene:*

> Fair Helen, the fairest living wight;
> Who in all godly thews and goodly praise
> Did far excel, but was most famous hight
> For skill in music of all in her days,
> As well in curious instruments as cunning lays.

There are several words you may not understand in this pretty verse. Helena is called 'the fairest living wight', that means the fairest living person; she has 'godly thews', that is godly qualities, or manners; and the line 'but was most famous hight' tells us that she was considered most famous as a musician.

There are some gold coins in the British Museum that were made, or struck, at the time our saint lived. On one of them is her portrait, with the names 'Flavia Helena Augusta' beneath it, meaning that she was an empress. Her face is long, with a very straight nose, big, full eyes, small lips closely pressed together, and a strong, round chin.

At Colchester there is an old paper, or document as it is generally called, given by King Henry the Fifth to the town, granting the people certain rights, on which an artist drew a picture of St Helena, wearing a crown, and long, flowing dress with a girdle set with precious stones. She holds a sceptre in her right hand. There is a high cross beside her, and on the scroll round her figure are the words in Latin:

'St Helena was born in Colchester. She was the mother of Constantine. Helena discovered the Holy Cross'.

There is another picture of the empress in the National Gallery by the painter called Fra Angelico. She is kneeling in the midst of angels who surround our Lord. Her hands are lightly held together in prayer; a cross rests in the bend of her left arm and leans against her shoulder. Her face is oval in shape, sweet and calm.

Yet another painting by the artist Paolo Veronese, also in the National Gallery, shows her asleep – but she looks like a Venetian, not a Roman, lady – with the vision of the Cross, carried by two little cherubs, over her head.

Have you noticed that in all the pictures I have described there is always a cross painted with St Helena? I will tell you why. It is because she had become a Christian, and was believed to have found the True Cross – the Cross itself on which our Saviour, Jesus Christ, ended the life that He gave for us.

After the death of her husband, St Helena's son became the first Christian emperor. He is known to the world as Constantine the Great.

Now, St Helena loved her son very dearly, and he

proved himself worthy of her love. He was a powerful emperor, a famous soldier, a wonderful man altogether. He protected the Christians in his empire, doing everything he could to help his mother in the work of her life. This was the noble work of a Christian, and reached its height in the finding of the Cross.

Constantine poured the treasures of his wealth into his mother's hands when she wished to set out for the Holy Land. It was some time after the emperor himself had had a vision of the Cross in the sky, when he was marching with his army on Rome. It was a flaming Cross, with these words in Latin:

'By this sign, conquer'.

The journey to Jerusalem was very long and hard. The empress was no longer young, but she never spoke of weariness, or even felt it, in her burning desire to reach Calvary, where, as you know, our Lord had been crucified.

Do not think that she neglected, for all her haste, to help her fellow-beings. No! Wherever she stopped the poor blessed her, for she gave alms – freely, gladly, with love in the giving – ordered the release of ill-used prisoners, visited the sick, cheered and consoled the unhappy. She built churches too, and adorned the shrine of many a saint.

It is said that an angel from Heaven told St Helena

where to search for the True Cross. The workmen dug into the earth, while their royal and gentle lady prayed beside them. Three wooden crosses were found, Jesus had been nailed upon one, two thieves upon the others.

St Helena was sorely troubled, and she sent for a very pious bishop named Macarius.

'How am I to tell the Cross of our Blessèd Lord from the other two?' she pleaded.

'We will trust in God to show us', he replied.

So they took the three to the house of a good woman who was very ill. Her friends were gathered round her bed, for they thought that she would die.

St Helena and the bishop touched her with the first cross, but there was no change. Her eyes were closed. She hardly seemed to breathe.

They touched her with the second cross. She did not move. Her skin was as white as snow.

They touched her with the third cross....

She lifted her head from the pillow. Her face was flushed with colour. She clasped her hands over her beating heart. She rose from her bed. She was healed!

It was in this way, by a miracle, they knew on which Cross our Lord had suffered.

St Helena built churches at Calvary and Bethlehem. Before leaving Jerusalem she gave a great banquet to young maidens, and waited upon them herself.

The True Cross was left in Jerusalem, but in later

years it was divided into many pieces and sent to different countries. The Emperor Constantine gave a precious fragment to the city of Rome, which St Helena herself took there. Two of the nails of the Cross she had also given to her son. One was put into the bridle of his horse, the other he placed in his crown.

There is a legend that when St Helena crossed the Adriatic Sea she was told of the great storms that so often swept over it. Many a brave ship had been lost with all her crew.

St Helena threw one of the nails into the water, in the name of Him who walked upon the waves and stilled their anger. It is said that the Adriatic has been more gentle and safe ever since.

St Helena lived to a great age, beloved and honoured. When the time came for her earthly crown to be laid aside she passed out of the world very peacefully, with her dear son, Constantine, holding her hand. She begged him, almost with her last breath, to protect Christianity and justice. The emperor caused his mother to be buried in a grand tomb built of the rock called porphyry, and raised a statue to her memory.

The Empress Helena was a noble lady. Do you know the true meaning of that word – lady? It is the loaf-giver, or one who offers bread to the hungry in love and kindness. To be noble is not to be rich, or proud, but honourable, true, worthy. To be a queen, as she was a queen, is not only to wear a crown and jewels, but to serve the people, help and educate them.

Last and greatest of all – far greater than the title of empress – she was a saint.

SAINT ALBAN

Fourth Century
Festival ⚜ June 22nd

Unbounded is the might
Of martyrdom, and fortitude, and right.
— William Wordsworth

ST ALBAN was the proto-martyr of Britain. That means he was the very first of the noble army of martyrs who died for our Saviour in this country. His name has come down to us through the ages. Let us make up our minds, all of us, not to forget it.

Everything is changed in England since the noble Alban lived and died.

Think! The language has changed, the laws, the customs, the clothes, the houses. Even the people of his race – the mighty Romans – rule us no more. The Danes, the Saxons, the Normans, where are they? We are all English today. We are all Britons.

When we remember this, and read the history of the past, it is wonderful to know that the name of a man like St Alban is with us still.

He was not a great king, or a great churchman. He

did not seek for honours or dream of fame. He was a simple, brave Christian, who saw the Light of the World when it first shone upon our land, like a star on a dark night. Other men could not see it. So it was that our saint won the palm of martyrdom and victory.

To begin at the beginning, there was a city called Verulam, at the time when Britain was held by the Romans, built in Hertfordshire where the little town of St Albans now stands.

It was surrounded by strong walls, and the country about it was wild and marshy. The winding river, to which the Romans gave its name of Ver, followed a different course then. It was a wide and lovely stream.

Although it is less than five-and-twenty miles from the heart of London, it is still possible, even today, to follow the River Ver to lonely places, where forget-me-nots grow on its banks, and one can see the bright wings of the kingfisher flash over the water.

I wish I could tell you the legend of St Alban in such a spot. There, looking over the elms and poplars, the oaks and beeches, as they grow today, we should see the distant roof and tower of his abbey. Alas, it is no longer the beautiful abbey that the children of two or three hundred years ago were taught to love. Even those children never saw the church, or the country itself, as it looked when St Alban's name was well known and honoured by the pious people of the long, long past.

Among the Romans who lived in the city, close to the outer walls, was a young noble, rich, happy, light-hearted; the son of an old family; the master of many servants; the owner of lands, horses, chariots, handsome clothes, golden plates, finely wrought drinking cups, gay curtains of soft colours – everything he wished that wealth could buy.

His name was Alban, and, although he enjoyed his easy life, the noble youth was quite unspoilt. He was kind, generous, frank, lovable. His greatest pleasure was to welcome guests to his house. He was not a Christian, for he had never heard the name of Christ, but he had the open mind and gentle heart of one who was ready for a perfect faith.

There were Christian churches in Britain, although it was long before the time when St Augustine of Canterbury – whose life you will read in a coming chapter – had sailed over the sea to preach to the people.

The Roman rulers worshipped their own gods, refusing to listen to the few wise men who had heard of the religion of our Lord.

Young Alban, living away from the court, knew nothing of these things. If he thought of God at all it was in a strange, uncertain way, as one gropes along a dark passage longing for a hand to guide him.

One night St Alban was told by his servants that there was an unknown guest at the door. He bade them bring him in.

The stranger was a man in the long, heavy robe of a priest. He walked slowly, leaning on his staff. Sun and wind had tanned his face dark brown. His hair hung upon his shoulders. He was old, but so worn and weary that he looked even older than his years.

So much St Alban saw at a first glance. Directly he looked in the face of the priest, and their eyes met, he forgot the rough clothes, the poorly shod feet, the hard, weather-beaten, weather-stained poverty of the whole figure.

It was a rugged face, but strong and tender. St Alban looked, standing before him, like a fine statue, glittering with gold and purple and precious stones.

'Thou art welcome!' said the Roman youth; 'tell me thy name and from whence thou comest'.

The unknown guest answered in a low voice, so that the servants could not hear his words.

'I fear to tell thee my name or from whence I come. I am flying from those who hate and would slay me. God forgive them!'

'Dost thou pray to God to forgive thine enemies?' cried Alban.

The priest laid a hand upon his arm.

'Wilt thou shelter me tonight, fair youth? I will tell

thee of One who died to save the souls of His enemies'.

Amazed, and greatly moved by his earnestness, Alban told the servants to bring food and wine and leave them together.

The priest, whose name was Amphibalus, talked with St Alban far into the night. He told him of the life and death of our Lord, and how, on the third day, He rose from the dead and passed into Heaven.

As the young Roman listened to the holy man his heart was uplifted. Tears of joy and gratitude filled his eyes. He did not doubt, or fear, or question. He was like the apostles – the first followers of Jesus – for he had faith on the instant.

Amphibalus knelt and thanked God, for he could read the deep, true nature of the young man. He forgot his own danger. He felt like a man who had found a long-lost son.

When Alban slept, a few hours before dawn, he dreamed a wonderful dream.

He saw, like a great picture being painted before his eyes, the Resurrection, or the rising of our Lord from the grave. He felt that an angel from Heaven had been sent to show it to him, and he knew that the One who had died for His enemies would never desert His friends.

The priest and Alban talked all through the following

day of the new and true religion. They left the house, so that the servants could not overhear them, and paced the broad lands bounded by the city walls.

When the old man was tired, at sunset, Alban took him home.

As they sat down to supper there was a sudden loud noise in the outer court. Alban thought that it was some of his friends, who knew that a feast and wine were always ready for them in that house. But the hunted priest started up, his eyes turned towards the door.

'Be not afraid', said his host; 'I will protect thee, holy Father'.

The noise grew louder. There was the tramp of heavy feet, the clash of arms, the hoarse voices of angry men. Then the door of the room burst open, and an old servant, who had known and loved Alban all his life, hurried in and closed it behind him.

'My lord!' he cried, 'soldiers are without – they say we have sheltered a Christian priest' and he stopped, gasping and pointing towards Amphibalus.

The old man clasped his hands in prayer.

'Give him up, my lord', said the man at the door; 'give him up or we shall all be lost!'

Amphibalus turned to Alban. He saw there was a bright smile on his face and his eyes were sparkling.

'Alban! wilt thou give me up to certain death?'

'No! Death shall be mine – and eternal life!'

With these words, putting forth the quick strength of his youth, St Alban stripped the rough, torn robe of the priest off his body and wrapped him hastily in his own rich cloak. It fell from shoulder to heel in gleaming folds of purple and red.

'Away – away by the western doors! God be with thee!' said the noble youth.

For one moment the priest paused, but the next, mastered by a courage greater than his own, he fled from the room and from the house. The servants let him pass, for they thought it was their master.

Alban put on the priest's robe and drew the hood down over his face.

'My lord!' gasped the old servant who loved him.

Alban lifted his hand and touched his lips, and even as he did so the soldiers rushed into the room.

They seized upon him. He was thrown to the ground. They dragged him along the floor, down the stairs, out into the night. He spoke no word, and he held his hands over his face, so that even his own men did not know him.

Amphibalus was saved, but there is an old story that he died the death of a martyr in after years. He never saw Alban again in this world. We trust and believe that they met where 'the wicked cease from tumult, and the wearied in strength are at rest'.

  Our saint was taken before the Roman governor of the country.
'What is thy name?' was the first question.
'Alban am I called'.
'Art thou of noble birth?'
'No; I am a servant'.
'Who is thy master?'
'The Lord Jesus Christ'.
'Dost thou worship the gods Jupiter and Apollo?'
'No; I worship the Lord Jesus Christ'.
'Wilt thou sacrifice and pray to Jupiter and Apollo?'
'No; I will sacrifice and pray to no false gods'.
The Roman governor looked at him long and steadily.
'Thou art young and handsome. If thou wilt kneel to our gods and serve them thou shalt be my guest, not my prisoner. I will give thee gold and silver. Thou shalt marry the fair daughter of a rich man'.
'No; I serve the Lord Jesus Christ. I will not take thy gifts or marry the fair daughter of a rich man. I will live only for my Lord'.
'Thou shalt die!' cried the Roman governor in fury.
'Thank God! How gladly, how proudly will I die for Him', said Alban.
The Roman governor was troubled. The people knew and loved Alban for his generosity, and he was half

afraid to treat him ill. Another man might have escaped, but Alban spoke against the gods and broke their images. He refused to do them lip-service. He longed for the crown of martyrdom.

St Alban was condemned to death, but the common people wept for him. He was so young and fair.

With soldiers on either side, with soldiers before and behind, he was marched from prison to the banks of the River Ver. There was a crowd upon the only bridge to see him pass. The soldiers could not force their way through the sorrowing men and women.

'Where wouldst thou take me?' said the prisoner.

'To yonder hill', said the leader of the soldiers.

'Am I to die on yonder hill?'

'Thou art to die'.

Then St Alban raised his hand and the first of three miracles took place.

The waters of the river rolled apart, leaving a dry path for the soldiers and their victim. Slowly they crossed to the opposite bank. Slowly they climbed the steep hill.

The grass was hot under their feet. The sunshine poured down, like a sheet of fire.

'I beg you', said St Alban, 'give me a cup of water, for I am parched with thirst'.

They laughed at him and refused.

Then the second miracle took place.

A cool, clear spring bubbled out of the earth. He stooped and made a cup of his two hands and drank and was refreshed.

The headsman, with his sharp axe, was ready. As the prisoner gazed upon him sadly, but not with anger, the third miracle took place.

It is said that the man's eyes dropped from his head. I think it means that he dared not look upon the holy face – its beauty blinded him with tears, for we are told that the cruel headsman lived to repent and love our Lord.

Then the soldiers drew their swords. Another executioner was thrust forward. The sharp axe rose – it flashed – it fell.

So it was that the first Christian saint of Britain, Alban, won the glory of a martyr's crown.

The noble Roman was not forgotten by those who came after him. A little church was built over his grave, but in later years a building of 'fine workmanship and suitable to Blessèd Alban's martyrdom' took its place. This was ruined by the Saxons, but one of their many kings, Offa, king of the Mercians, honoured St Alban above all the other saints of Britain. His memory was also beloved by the Danes.

The old city of Verulam has long borne his name.

Many poets have sung and written his story. Artists used to paint him in armour, but there is no good reason to believe he was a soldier.

There is an old saying that 'the blood of the martyrs is the seed of the Church'. Remember this if you go to the town of St Albans.

You will see the remains, overgrown with grass, of the Roman walls. You will see the abbey, built on the spot where St Alban died. You will be able to wander along the British causeway, where the branches of the trees meet overhead, like the roof of a great cathedral, with sunbeams quivering and shaking through them.

Then, as you hear the bells of the abbey in the distance, and watch the doves and busy jackdaws circling round its tower, think of the brave St Alban, who saved the life of his friend and died for the sake of his Lord.

ST GEORGE

SAINT GEORGE

Fourth Century
Festival ✦ April 23rd

For thou, amongst those saints whom thou dost see,
Shalt be a saint, and thine own nation's friend
And patron: thou Saint George shalt called be,
Saint George of merry England, the sign of victory.
  — Edmund Spenser

'Now there was a young man whose name was George, sun of truth and the glorious star betwixt Heaven and earth'.

This sentence, from an old book, is a fitting foreword for the story of our own St George.

You know why I call him our own St George? Of course you do! But I wonder whether you can think of the many, many ways in which his name is woven into our lives today?

To begin with, he is the patron saint of England. We see his red cross on the national flag of our country. The English red rose is worn in his honour. One of the oldest orders of chivalry in Europe is the Order of the Knights of St George, although it is generally called the Order of the Garter. There are nearly two hundred churches dedicated to his memory.

I hope you will never forget that the famous naval raid on Zeebrugge, in the fourth year of the Great War, took place on the eve of St George's Day in April. It was one of the most daring deeds in the history of our glorious navy, and the admiral's message that flashed across the sea was the old, undying battle-cry:

'St George for England!'

That is the battle-cry of our hearts. It makes us think of many a famous field. I am sure you will read some day – if you have not read it now – Shakespeare's story of the victorious fight upon St Crispin's Day, when Henry the Fifth of England ends his great speech to his troops:

> Follow your spirit: and, upon this charge,
> Cry 'God for Harry! England! and St George!'

There are so many things for you to know about St George.

Above everything else, he is our ideal soldier. Many great saints have been soldiers – St Theodore, for instance, and St Florian – but St George is the greatest of all. Shall I tell you some of the titles which have been given to him?

Captain of the Noble Army of Martyrs.

The Victorious Commander.

SAINT GEORGE

The Trophy Bearer.
Le Chevalier de la Belle Monture.

The last is his favourite name in France, meaning 'the Knight of the Beautiful Steed', for he is generally associated with a noble horse.

There is another thing to notice in the pictures, medals, or statues of St George. He is always represented as very fair to look upon – a lovely knight, young, strong, radiant – with a hideous dragon dying, or dead, at his feet.

Now, St George lived such a long, long time ago that it is very hard to find out his story. So many books and poems have been written about him. There is one that I hope you will read with great delight some day, for it is in our own language, while another I am thinking of that would give you a better idea of his life is in Latin and strangely told.

The English poem was written by Edmund Spenser, who lived in the time of Queen Elizabeth the First.

It is called *The Faerie Queene,* and begins by telling us 'a gentle knight was pricking on the plain'; he is the Knight of the Red Cross, and his noble adventure is to rescue a lovely lady from 'a dragon horrible and stern'. So begins the well-known legend of St George.

In the course of St George's wanderings he came to a fair city where the king and people were most unhappy. A monstrous dragon had come forth from the waters of the deep and demanded, as tribute, or a gift, the life of a youth or maiden.

You can imagine the dismay, the grief, the fear of the wretched people. They dared not approach the river, without the city walls, where the horrible dragon waited to devour its prey.

They were in despair.

The king's only daughter, Cleodolinda – Edmund Spenser calls her by the more beautiful name of Una – offered to be sacrificed to the dragon to save the poor people whom she loved.

You can well imagine the breaking heart of the king; the tears of her friends; the crowded streets through which she passed; the sounds of mingled horror and great relief as the men and women saw her go by – pity for her youth and beauty, joy at their own deliverance, pride in her courage, wonder at her meek and gentle spirit.

Mothers clasped their young daughters in their arms and wept. Fathers looked from their children's sweet faces to the sweet face of the princess, and shuddered to think of the dragon.

It was all so sad and dreadful.

Then, into the midst of that unhappy scene, like a burst of glorious sunshine in the darkness of a stormy sky, the Red Cross Knight rode into the city.

SAINT GEORGE

He was clad in armour, his keen lance in his hand, with the sign of his dear Lord upon his breastplate. In the words of the poet of *The Faerie Queene:*

Upon his shield the like was also scor'd,
For sovereign help which in His help he had.
Right faithful true he was in deed and word.

Of course the people crowded round him. He heard the dreadful reason of their misery. He saw the fair princess who was to be sacrificed to the monster.

Here was an adventure to stir his brave heart and nerve his strong hand! So he bade the king and people be of good cheer, and instead of the beautiful maiden the equally beautiful youth went forth to meet the dragon. 'Right faithful true he was in deed and word'.

Then came the greatest fight ever fought.

The monster was stretched upon a great hill – himself like a hill. He was covered with brass scales that clashed with a terrible sound as he moved; his loose, drooping wings were like sails fluttering feebly in a breeze; his huge, long tail was wound into a hundred folds, spotted with red and black, sweeping all the land behind him, with two deadly stings at its points, but even these were as nothing compared to the sharpness of his cruel, rending claws.

It is difficult to describe his hideous head, with jaws gaping wide and three rows of iron teeth, half hidden in the clouds of his smoky, burning breath. His eyes blazed in hatred.

He lifted his great spotted breast as the Red Cross Knight approached him, and roared so terribly that the echoes were awakened far and near.

The knight dashed forward and attacked the monster with his steady spear, but the pointed steel was turned aside by the brass scales, and with one sweep of the long tail both man and horse were thrown to the ground.

St George leapt up, remounted, and charged at him again – again without avail, but the great force of the blow so enraged the dragon that he suddenly beat the air with his wide, ungainly wings. Lifting his body off the ground he seized St George and his steed with his grasping claws and bore him high into the air, like a hawk with a helpless bird.

The knight struggled so violently that the monster could not hold him, and, plunging towards the earth, he was obliged to let him go. As they dropped together, pell-mell, the swift, glittering spear caught the monster under the left wing, leaving a gaping wound in his neck.

He roared and struggled to drag out the spear, but it broke in his flesh, and he threw himself against the shield of the knight, who drew his sword and hacked at the terrible claws.

Fire and smoke rushed from the monster's mouth.

The knight staggered backwards – choking, blinded – but unconquered. Behind him was a clear, deep stream, beneath the shade of a leafy tree. As he fell into the water, and it splashed over him, he was instantly refreshed and his wounds made whole.

The daylight had begun to fade. He stretched his aching and bruised limbs in welcome repose. The sun set and he fell asleep, bathed in the soft evening air and cool water.

On the following day the fight went on.

The monster, terrified to see again the recovered knight, whom he had supposed to be killed, rushed upon him in fury and despair. St George thrust his bright sword into the open jaws with all the strength of his mighty arm.

The life of the wicked fiend rushed out of his mouth; the ground shook under his writhing body; clouds of his smoky breath darkened the air; he plunged and roared, roared and plunged; his scaly wings rose and flapped more and more feebly.

At last, like a huge rocky cliff torn from the mainland in a tempest, he crashed and fell and lay upon the earth, dead.

So runs the legend of St George and the dragon. Every legend, as I told you in the life of St Christopher, has a deeper meaning than the mere telling of a tale.

The Red Cross Knight is meant to represent holiness; the fair maiden for whom he fought is the Christian Church, and the terrible monster who threatened to devour him is the power of evil.

In other words, he is the knight of virtue with sin under his heel.

You will often hear our saint called St George of Cappadocia. That is the name of the place in Asia Minor where some people say he was born. Others think his home was in Palestine.

His father was a soldier in the service of a powerful emperor, but he died when George was a boy, and he lived with his mother, who was a lady of great wealth.

St George became a soldier himself when he was seventeen, and found such favour in the eyes of the emperor that he was quickly promoted to a post of high honour.

This was a time of great storm and stress for Christians, as the emperor despised the true faith and treated the followers of our Lord with great cruelty.

The young soldier was moved to pity, for he understood and felt the appeal of the Christian religion. His protests, when he tried to help the Christians, were mocked at, or ignored, and he was seriously warned by his companions not to offend the emperor.

Now, St George was of high birth, and very rich

in money and estates. He thought of the words our Saviour had spoken to another man of great possessions: 'Give to the poor...and come follow Me'.

So he freed his slaves, gave away everything he possessed – even his own handsome clothes and suits of armour – and openly declared himself a Christian.

The emperor, as St George had been warned, was very angry and tried to induce his favourite to worship his own false gods. When he refused – meekly, but with inner courage as great as any he had ever shown on the battlefield – the emperor tried to subdue him with harsh threats, followed by imprisonment and merciless tortures.

St George was upheld in his agony, not only by his trust and love of his Lord, but by the blessing of a voice from Heaven:

'George, fear nothing. I am with thee!'

All the unspeakable cruelties he suffered after that were powerless to break his spirit. Even the emperor was moved to wonder by his courage. Even his torturers trembled before him. A faith they could never understand – a faith that was stronger than all their wicked force – lived in the heart of the dying martyr.

It was a faith that never failed him, a light that never grew dim, a hope that never passed away. So he died, the Red Cross Knight, the soldier of Christ, the model and type of a perfect hero.

Now, I want to tell you how and why the Captain of the Noble Army of Martyrs became the patron saint of England.

King Edward the Confessor was our patron saint until the reign of Richard the First.

Edward was the last of the Saxon kings to rule this country, and was famous for his justice and piety. He it was who built Westminster Abbey – 'a church of St Peter in the thorny islet of the River Thames' – and it is there he was buried. So it is well to remember that our patron saint, before St George, was an English king, whose rule, it was said, was so just 'that the people lived in Christian love and godly fear'.

When Richard the First, called the Lion-hearted, succeeded to the throne, one hundred and twenty-three years after the Norman conquest, he led the crusaders overseas to fight for the Holy Land.

During one of his fiercest battles, when the English were in sore distress and nearly conquered, King Richard prayed for the help of the great soldier saint, George.

It is said that a knight in full armour, dazzling and beauteous as the sunshine, instantly appeared riding a white horse. A wave of hope and courage swept over the field. The despair and threatened flight of the soldiers were changed to fortitude and fiery resolution.

They turned upon the pagan enemy, the Red Cross

Knight at their head, and drove him before them like chaff before the wind.

'St George for England!' they shouted.

In the moment of victory the dazzling champion, on his white steed, vanished from before their eyes. King Richard, thanking God for the triumph of his arms, vowed that his soldier saint should henceforth be honoured as the patron of our country.

While the veneration that was paid to him reached its greatest height in the reign of our most noble soldier king, Henry the Fifth, he has never lost his hold over the English people.

In the time of King Henry the Eighth there was a piece of money called a George noble, and his figure has been stamped on our golden sovereigns to this day. Even in that far land on the other side of the world, Australia, they have chosen the emblem of the ideal Christian knight to adorn their finest coins.

We live in a time of history, when the banner of our patron saint has been raised in all parts of the world. The symbol of the Cross that he bore on his breastplate – 'The sign of his dear Lord' – means that divine pity, in the sadness and sorrow of war, is still alive and will ever live.

The Red Cross is lifted in the battlefield; it floats over the ships that bring our wounded heroes home; it is unfurled to the soft winds of Heaven at havens of rest and healing; it is the pledge of our sympathy with those who suffer; it holds the promise of a better world.

The perfect knight was a great soldier, but he drew his sword only in defence of the injured. It was the spirit of evil that he conquered, no earthly foe, for he was merciful and gentle.

St George for England!

SAINT NICHOLAS

Fourth Century
Festival ⚜ December 6th

Our roses bloom and fade away,
Our Infant Lord abides alway.
May we be blessed His face to see
And ever little children be.
— Hans Christian Andersen

THIS is the story of the saint whom you should love best of all. He belongs to you. He is your very own. I do not believe there is one among you – even if you are now too big to enjoy yourselves at all in the old way – who will not admit that he gave you pleasure and delight in those far-off days when you were really little.

You all remember St Nicholas! How anxiously you waited for his rare visits! You believed that he came to see you once a year on Christmas eve. It was a very good belief, and you must not think, if you have outgrown it, that it was rather foolish of you and perhaps a little deceitful in other people to teach you to believe it.

No! Your expectation of Santa Claus – for that is the name by which you know St Nicholas – is the children's way of keeping his memory green. Whether you think of him as coming down the chimney in the middle of the night, or rushing through the silent streets in a sledge drawn by reindeer, really does not matter. But there was a time when St Nicholas lived in this world, not in Lapland, where his reindeer come from, nor in the towns where his toys are made.

His real home was in a place called Lycia, in Asia Minor. Being the son of a very rich man, and dearly loved by his father and mother, Nicholas's life must have been very easy and pleasant, and, had he not possessed a strong will and great fervour, no doubt he would have passed his time as idly and aimlessly as many another boy, only thinking of the bright opportunities of youth when youth is over.

St Nicholas had no desire for money to spend upon himself. He disliked, at the same time, to be thanked when he gave it away. Even in his babyhood he had surprised his parents by his wise little sayings. They thought him, later on, a very strange boy. No doubt, when he grew up, few of his friends understood his nature, much as they all loved him.

He did not care for ordinary pleasures; he never dreamed of winning fame; he was quite indifferent to sports or gaiety; oddly enough, some people thought, he sought the society of children, and preferred it to any other.

I wish we could talk to the children who knew St Nicholas. They would be able to tell us much about him, but I do not think the description of any one can give one the same impression of a person as one's own eyes and ears.

St Nicholas was far more than an eccentric, open-handed youth. (Eccentric, you know, is another word for odd, being unlike other people.) His love of beauty and joy of living was as great as that of any of his friends, but with this difference.

He worshipped the beauty of a noble life; he was proud to be the most humble servant of our Saviour; his joy in this world was to make himself ready, by prayer and work, for the next.

The virtue of charity must have appealed, perhaps more than any other, to the heart of our saint. This is shown in many of the pictures of Old Masters, for some of the most famous artists in the past painted St Nicholas.

There is one in our National Gallery by the great Raphael, and another in Rome by the divine painter Fra Angelico. He is generally drawn holding a book and – in allusion to the story of his best-known charity that I am now going to tell you – with three golden balls or three purses.

There was a certain noble, living near the home of St Nicholas, who was too poor to give a dowry to either of his three fair daughters.

That was very sad for him, for it was a strict custom for every young girl, when she was old enough to be married, to receive this gift from her father. You can imagine how the poor man grieved, and the girls, although they tried to hide it from him, felt very sorry too.

I do not know whether any one of them was engaged to be married, but I expect they thought about it now and then. They were quite young and very fond of one another. They lived in a quaint, quiet house.

When the girls had gone to bed at night in an inner room – they slept side by side with their little heads in a straight line on the same pillow, as you will see some day in the picture – the father would sit and think about his poverty in the outer room. He rested his brow on his hand and looked very miserable.

St Nicholas had heard all about it. He did not smile unkindly, as some people would have done, or pity the family and forget them five minutes afterwards. He resolved to help. So what do you think he did?

Go to see the father to give him good advice? Tell the girls that if they had no dowries they had better make up their minds to stay unmarried? Offer to give them a present, with a great show of generosity and much talk?

Not at all! He did not say a word to anybody. In the

middle of the night, half hidden in the folds of a dark cloak, he stealthily approached the quaint, quiet house, stood on tip-toe to peep through the open window, and threw in a purse of gold as a dowry for the eldest of the sisters.

On the following night he threw in an equally heavy bag of gold for the second sister. So far his secret was safe. No one had seen him, or noticed his absence from home.

On the third night, after lightly tossing the handsome gift for the youngest sister through the window, he was about to steal away when the door of the house burst open, the father ran out and caught him by the cloak.

'Nicholas!' he cried, recognising the young man; 'why dost thou hide thy generosity? I have been watching and waiting all through the night!'

So it became known, much to the saint's distress, for he could not deny the truth.

The three little maidens were even more pleased than their father. I expect they were soon married, having such rich dowries, and lived happily ever after.

Perpetually giving away his possessions, St Nicholas himself lived in poverty, hiding his good deeds and bestowing his gifts, whenever it was possible, in the darkness and silence of night.

He became very well known to the people, who loved him as much for his kindness and simplicity as for his constant services. He lived alone, after the manner of holy men of those far-off days, giving much time to prayer and praise of God.

St Nicholas never wished, or even thought of, the great change that was to come into his life.

A bishop had died, the Bishop of Myra, and the priesthood of that place could not decide upon his successor. They were in great trouble and perplexity, for a bishop is a powerful man and much depends upon him.

They gathered together and prayed for guidance. Then a strange thought flashed into the mind of one of the priests. He felt as if a voice had whispered in his ear, giving counsel. So he rose from his knees and spoke to his companions.

This was his thought – or inspiration is a better word – that they should all go to a certain church at midnight, implore the help of God before the altar, and watch for the dawn. Then the first man who came in to offer his morning prayer would be their bishop chosen by Heaven.

The priests rejoiced in this holy thought. They arranged to go to a little, quiet church on the high road.

They prayed long and earnestly, waiting for the blessèd light of morning. All their thoughts must have been with the future bishop, whoever he might be. Perhaps they believed – who knows? – that some famous churchman would be the first to come. Perhaps they longed for a very gifted preacher.

Slowly the night passed away. As the faint clouds of dawn drifted over the sky, they saw, against the open door, the dark figure of a man. Their hearts beat high. They withdrew into the shadow of the wall and watched.

He advanced with a dragging step, as if he were very tired; but on nearing the altar his manner changed. He raised his drooping head, hurried forward, and threw himself upon his knees with joy and reverence.

Behold! It was simple Brother Nicholas, returning homeward after one of his secret deeds of charity.

At first he refused the high office of bishop; but after a little while, believing that it was the will of God, he consented to accept it, and ruled in justice and peace till the end of his life.

While we are talking of our saint being Bishop of Myra, I must tell you of a curious old custom that has long since passed away.

On St Nicholas's Day, December 6, the choristers of certain churches were allowed to choose a 'boy bishop', who reigned over them for three weeks like a little king. During that time the children arranged little pageants and games in honour of all other children beloved by the good St Nicholas. It was a pretty way of amusing themselves, and I do not know why you should not try to play at something of the kind in your own homes. What do you think?

St Nicholas never came to England. But he is said to have travelled by sea many times. He went to the Holy Land, and it was during that journey he became the patron saint of all good mariners.

One night there was a great storm. All the crew knew they were in great danger. Several believed their last hour had come.

St Nicholas was calm and steadfast in the midst of tumult. He prayed aloud, offering their souls to God if it was His will that their bodies were to perish, but entreating Him to spare their lives for a little longer that they might repent of their sins and learn to know Him better. He prayed that their little ship might weather the storm for the sake of Him who stilled the waves of the sea and rebuked the wind.

His prayer was answered. The tempest ended. They reached port in safety, and all the sailors, when he blessed them and bade them farewell, begged him to remember them every day in his holy prayers.

There are other stories of his affection for brave sailors, and that is the reason, I do not doubt, that his name first became well known and deeply honoured in this island of ours. The English are a seafaring people – we all of us love the sea – and there have been hundreds of churches dedicated to him, chiefly in our seaport towns, such as Yarmouth, Liverpool, and Whitehaven.

There are two more stories of St Nicholas's good deeds I want to tell you before we bid him good-bye.

It came to his knowledge, when he was Bishop of Myra, that three travellers unknown to the country had been accused of a crime and sent to prison.

He went to see them, and quickly discovered that their trial had been most unfair. They were perfectly innocent men condemned to death.

Nicholas was filled with horror at such injustice and pitied them with all his heart. It was not in his power to save them by ordinary means, but he knew that God would help him.

What do you think happened? The legend tells us that he appeared before the emperor of the country in a dream, told him of the poor travellers, and bade him be merciful as he hoped for mercy.

So the Emperor gave orders that the innocent men should be set at liberty, and the bishop bade them depart in peace.

The second of these stories is nearly always told, or shown by a quaint old drawing, in books about the saints.

When Nicholas was travelling through his diocese – that means the part of the country of which he was bishop – he came to a small tavern. It was kept by a very wicked man who pretended, nevertheless, to be kind and hospitable, and always welcomed his guests cheerfully.

I hardly like to tell you what he did, but you must remember it happened a long time ago and it is a legend, that is to say, there is an inner meaning to the story. Well, this cruel landlord persuaded little children to come into his house and he killed them, for the purpose of giving them to his guests to eat, just like the giant is supposed to do in a fairy tale.

Directly the gentle St Nicholas went into the tavern, where he was to sup and sleep, he felt that it was not a good place, in spite of the host's smiling welcome. At first the bishop did not speak of his impression, but it became so strong, and made him so unhappy, that he was sure a dreadful deed had been committed in the house.

He prayed for help to find it out, and, directly afterwards, he noticed a big tub in a dark corner. Without saying a word he went towards it, still praying silently, and made the Sign of the Cross.

There was a sound of movement in the tub, and – I am so glad the bishop was in time! – the heads of three children slowly appeared, with their little hands uplifted in thankfulness. So they were saved from the cruel, cruel landlord and given back to their friends by our own loving St Nicholas.

The third legend has also a happy ending. A certain rich man and his wife were very anxious to have a little son, and often said to each other that if ever they had a child they would give a golden cup to a church named after St Nicholas, as a proof of their gratitude.

So, when a baby was born, the father caused the cup to be made by a skilful goldsmith, but I am sorry to tell you that he was so charmed with its beauty that he could not bear to part with it. So he broke his promise and kept the treasure for himself.

His little son grew into a handsome, brave boy, the delight of his eyes and the pride of his heart. One summer day, when they were out together, the father gave him the golden cup, with orders to fill it with water at the river and bring it back that the man might quench his thirst.

The boy took the cup and started to run on his errand, but alas! he never returned. He fell into the river, to his father's deep sorrow, and everybody believed that he was drowned.

Then the miserable man thought of his broken promise. The treasure he had prized so highly had gone with his son, but he took a silver cup instead – the best that he had – and laid it on the altar of the church, weeping and praying that he might be comforted by Heaven and forgiven.

O joy! He suddenly saw the lost child standing before him, alive and well, with the beautiful golden cup shining in his hand. It was St Nicholas who had saved him from death in the river.

Some people tell this story differently. They say that the boy was stolen by thieves and became a slave in a far-away country, where he served a heathen king. On St Nicholas's birthday the poor child wept bitter tears, and prayed that he might return to his home. His master jeered and mocked him, but the Christian saint, friend of every good child, restored him that very night to his own people. The gentle St Nicholas is honoured by the Church on the sixth of December, eighteen days before small boys and girls expect him to bring them their Christmas presents.

They may still look forward to Santa Claus, for he is sure to come.

Bigger children should not forget him. All we know of him shows us a saint indeed – kind, holy, charitable, inspired by devotion to the glory of God.

SAINT AMBROSE

Fourth Century
Festival — December 7th

God shall be my hope,
My stay, my guide, and lantern to my feet.
        — William Shakespeare

THERE was a noble Roman family, towards the end of that wonderful fourth century which gave us so many saints, to whom we should all look back with interest and affection. The father was named Ambrosius. He held a very high position in the empire, for he was the governor of important places in foreign lands that were under the rule of the Roman emperors. The mother was of a sweet and pious nature, lovable and kind.

There were three children, named Marcellina, Satynus and Ambrose. They were not only fond of one another, as brothers and sisters are, but there was a feeling of unusual sympathy added to their love. I mean that they were patient with each other's differences of taste and temper in trifling matters, for at heart they always agreed. The girl was some years older than the boys. Both she and Satynus knew that Ambrose was more sensitive and thoughtful than they were. Without putting it into words, they felt that his nature was so lofty and earnest that they did not quite understand him.

No doubt he was often happy and gay like other children, and joined in their games; but at times he seemed to be lost in thought, and then he would look so beautiful that they were surprised and stole away on tiptoe, leaving him alone.

There never was any human being more closely drawn into the communion of saints than Ambrose in after years, and even as a child he felt the joy and wonder of the nearness of God. We know that He is always with us, if we will but listen for His voice in our hearts. Ambrose heard it more clearly than other men.

He loved our Saviour with so great a love, he thought of our Saviour's Holy Mother and the saints of the Church with such a depth of feeling, that his whole life was like a long prayer. He was a saint himself, but never dreamed, in his meekness, of being numbered among the blessèd.

In spite of the many struggles and hardships of his life, for few men have had to fight for Christianity as he did, St Ambrose remained calm, peaceful, unchanged by the storm and stress of his work in the world.

Even his name – Ambrose – is a soft and gentle

word. He spoke so sweetly that a legend tells how the bees, when he was an infant, had flown round his head and touched his lips with their honey. For that reason many of the great Italian artists painted a beehive in their pictures of him.

St Augustine wrote of St Ambrose: 'He was one of those who speak the truth, and speak it well, pointedly, and with beauty and power of words'.

But let us go back to our saint's boyhood.

His father Ambrosius, the noble Roman governor, died when St Ambrose was about ten years old. His mother returned to her old home, near the city of Rome, with the three children. Marcellina helped her to look after the two boys. She was a quiet girl, content to stay in the house, as pious as her mother, and devoted to her brothers.

They were well educated, and it was settled that Ambrose, perhaps on account of his gift for public speaking, should study law.

I need not tell you about the work that he did in the first busy years after he left home. It is enough to say that he soon became well known and held several high posts, as his father had done before him.

Then a time came when he was governor of the great city of Milan in northern Italy. The bishop had lately died, and it was agreed that the people should gather together to choose their new bishop.

It was a big meeting of anxious, eager men and women, for there had been troublous times in the Church owing to heresy, or false ideas, among a certain number of people in the country.

You can imagine the look of the crowd, in spite of the different clothes that they wore in those days, for all crowds are more or less alike. Some pressed roughly forward, pushing others aside with elbows and shoulders; some of the women were half frightened; some of the men quarrelled; there were the cries of children, the loud voices of noisy youths, the sound of a laugh now and then, and the buzz of everybody talking at the same time.

Even when there was silence in the throng, in readiness for the speakers, a murmur could still be heard on the outer edges, with the rustle and stir of movement.

Suddenly a voice rang out – loud, clear as a bell, piercingly sweet – the voice of a child.

'Ambrose – bishop!'

No one could tell from whence it came. All heard it. Every man looked at his neighbour to find his neighbour looking at him. What did it mean? How could their beloved governor be made a bishop? They all knew that he was not even a priest.

'Ambrose – bishop!'

Once more the child's clear note swept through the hall, but this time it was caught up and repeated by a hundred voices – a thousand – the whole multitude echoed the cry:

'Ambrose for our bishop! Ambrose! Ambrose!'

Nothing could stop them. No speaker could make them listen. They had chosen the just and true man in their midst.

Could he refuse the prayers of all his friends, known and unknown? No worldly wealth or honour would have moved him, but the call of his own people touched him to the heart. He believed that the will of God had been made clear. It was his duty to obey.

I cannot tell you the name of the one in the crowd who had cried 'Ambrose – bishop!' It may have been some child who saw him in the distance, knew his face, and repeated after his name the word that was in everybody's mouth – bishop. There is one old legend that it was the perfect Child Himself, Jesus, who knew Ambrose and loved him for his goodness.

The first act of our saint, after becoming a priest and Bishop of Milan, was to put all his money and other belongings into the hands of his brother Satynus, to be given, as they were needed, to the poor.

His dear sister, Marcellina, lived in the house he had owned when he was governor, but afterwards became a nun. Nothing could alter the affection of the three. For nearly forty years St Ambrose gave, and was given in return, the love and kindness which had started in their childhood and was never outgrown.

His own house was open to all, from the emperor to the beggar. I cannot tell you his full story, for it is said that to write a history of St Ambrose would mean writing a history of the Italy of his day.

He is one of the Fathers of the Church. The famous St Augustine, Bishop of Hippo, whose life you will find in another part of this book, held him very dear, and the people of Milan adored their *Sant'Ambrogio*.

He was as powerful as any king or ruler. In truth, there was an emperor named Theodosius – that is a name we call in English Theodore – who tried in vain to make the bishop obey his commands whether they were right or wrong. He was firmly refused, and a long struggle between them ended in the triumph of St Ambrose.

You must not think that he hated Theodosius after this. No, he was loyal to the emperor in everything that was right, and forgave him readily for his injustice.

St Ambrose was fond of music, as we have very good cause to remember, for he wrote the noble hymn that has been sung ever since his time in Christian churches, and will go on being sung for ages yet to come. It is called the *Te Deum Laudamus,* or 'Praise of God', and begins:

O God, we praise Thee:
We acknowledge Thee to be the Lord.
Everlasting Father,
All the earth doth worship Thee…

You will be interested to hear that St Ambrose is the patron of all domestic animals, our dogs and cats and other pets. He is supposed to protect geese, because the day on which the Church honours his memory is December 7th, and in Italy, the country where he was born, a goose is drawn in pictures of winter time. In England, as you know, we generally see a robin redbreast.

Many of the greatest Italian artists have made pictures of St Ambrose. I think the most beautiful idea of them all is to paint him with an angel whispering in his ear. It was meant to show that his thoughts were so pure and divine that our Lord must have sent them to him by the lips of a heavenly messenger.

St Ambrose did not live to be an old man. His last hours were very peaceful. He was writing on the 42nd Psalm when the end came – the end in this world, but the beginning of his life in the next.

The very beautiful words at the close of that Psalm must have given deep joy to the quiet spirit of this true saint:

Hope in God, for I will still give praise to Him:
The salvation of my countenance, and my God.

ST MARTIN OF TOURS

SAINT MARTIN OF TOURS

Fourth Century
Festival ⚔ November 11th

If we would endeavour like brave men to stand in the battle, surely we should behold above us the help of God from Heaven. For He Himself who giveth us occasions to fight, to the end we may get the victory, is ready to succour those who strive.
— Thomas à Kempis

ST MARTIN, Bishop of Tours, is one of the many soldier saints. His long story, briefly told, is that he lived in this world over eighty years, and it would fill the pages of a big book to describe all his life, the miracles he is believed to have performed, the friends who loved him, and the country where he dwelt.

St Martin at eighty years! It is hard to realise that our saint could ever grow old.

I always think of him as a young soldier – young and strong and valiant like St George – with the light of a new hope flashing in his eyes, his heart beating with new warmth, his soul lit up with a new faith.

His family was not Christian. Born in a little town

on the borders of Hungary in the fourth century, he was the son of a soldier, and passed his childhood in different places where his father's regiment was stationed.

Little is known of this famous saint's life as a boy, but it is said that he ran away from home, when he was only ten years old, to go into a monastery.

I need not tell you he was much too young; and you know it was not right to leave the house of his father and mother, for any reason, without their permission. But it shows us that the boy, young as he was, must have thought about leading a religious life, or talked to some one who had described it in a way he could understand.

In short, his childish action – thoughtless and foolish as it must have seemed to other people – was neither a whim nor merely love of strange adventures.

He had heard the call of his Master, but he was not old enough to answer it rightly, for his present duty was to stay at home, proving his loyalty to that Master by patience and obedience.

Martin was only fifteen when his father, determined he should never be a monk, arranged for him to join the emperor's army. As the son of a veteran, he was not only expected to desire the profession of arms, but obliged by custom and rule to become a soldier.

We are told in a life of St Martin – yes! these facts are taken from a book actually written by a friend of his hundreds of years ago – that he made a good officer, living so frugally on his pay that he had enough money to give away in charity.

He kept only one man and treated him more like a brother than a paid servant. His father, doubtless, was very well pleased with Martin's attention to his military duties, but I expect his comrades, boys of the same age, found him hard to understand.

Aimless pleasures did not attract him, but he was never dull. He seemed to possess an inner spring of deep, serious happiness, as if he were a soldier, not of the emperor whom they all obeyed, but of One who was far higher and more exacting, but so noble that to serve Him was the greatest of all honours, and to follow Him a happiness more than any man deserved.

We know that this was true of St Martin. He had chosen his Leader, although the time had not come to acclaim Him.

It was while the young soldier was still in the emperor's army, when he is supposed to have been quartered at the old French city of Amiens, that he dreamed one of the most beautiful and inspiring dreams that ever came to a man in a sleep of peace. It is a legend that has been told through the ages in poem and picture, interwoven with the life story of St Martin of Tours.

Can you draw this scene in your minds? It is a busy street in Amiens on a bright, frosty, winter morning.

We can see the people going to their work, or to market, with a little crowd here and there talking together, while the boys and girls were running along, loitering, laughing, behaving very much as they do today. There would be horsemen on the road; perhaps a rich lady would pass by, her armed servant at her heels; or a prosperous merchant, with his clerk beside him listening meekly to his master's orders.

Look! In a shadow of the city wall, as unheeded as a mound of dust, is a poor, ragged beggar, shivering with cold, one feeble hand stretched out for alms. The people pass him by, most of them ignoring him altogether, some with a glance of half-contemptuous pity, or even disgust.

His pleading voice is so weak that it fades away. He is utterly despised.

Suddenly there is the ring of horses' hoofs on the hard road, and a little band of the emperor's soldiers canter down the street. They are talking gaily among themselves; their swords, their big spurs, and the trappings of their steeds glisten in the sunshine. They are leaving for a distant city, and carelessly glance at the people who stand still to watch them pass, admiring their youth and gallant bearing.

As they pass by the shadow of the city wall one of the young officers, in the rear of the gay troop, reins in his horse.

What does he see? Why does his face change? There is nothing of interest to attract his attention, only a shuddering beggar with outstretched hands, and a haggard, starving face.

There is no money in young Martin's purse – he has given it all away in charity and farewell gifts – and he is sorely distressed at his poverty.

Then an idea flashes into his head, suggested by the cold wind that whistles through the air. He pulls off his big, warm cloak and tears it in half, stoops from the saddle to drop the bigger part over the shoulders of the wretched beggar with a word of sympathy, and gallops after his companions.

We can hear the mocking laughter and scornful jests of the other young officers as he joins them, with his strip of torn cloak fluttering behind him.

That night, in a happy dream, a vision of Heaven appeared to him. He saw the celestial hosts of the Lord, and in their midst – surrounded by light and colour more beautiful than even the skies of dawn – he saw our Saviour Himself, and lo! He was wrapped in a soldier's torn cloak!

Then Martin knew to whom he had stooped from the saddle and given his poor gift.

> Amen I say to you, as long as you did it to one of these my least brethren, you did it to me.

It was very soon after this time that St Martin openly declared himself a Christian, and was baptised.

He resolved to leave the army, but as it happened there was a campaign against the Germans about to be undertaken, and some of his comrades – perhaps wilfully – mistook the reason of his unexpected action. They declared he was a coward, afraid to meet an enemy in warfare.

St Martin was not angry, but he offered at once to go unarmed to the very front ranks to prove his courage. He would have been taken at his word, for no man ever doubted him, if peace had not been made before the campaign opened.

So he bade farewell to his old friends and his old life, and left them all behind him. He was very young, under twenty, and the hardest battles of his life were still to be fought.

Now, St Martin believed in great austerity. That means that he was strict, even harsh, with himself, giving up all comforts, doing the most severe penance for any sins he committed, and living alone in extreme poverty.

His first important act, after entering the Church, was to seek the counsel and help of a great Christian, St Hilary, who was then Bishop of Poitiers in France. They understood and liked each other at first meeting, and a lifelong friendship grew up between them.

Those were troublous times for the Church, but I do not think you would be interested in a description of heresies, or false beliefs. They did not alter the true Christianity of our saint's steadfast heart, but they had a great effect, nevertheless, on his outer life.

His beloved St Hilary was banished from France, and St Martin went to Milan, in Italy, for he would have felt very unhappy without him, and lived as a hermit for a long time.

Choosing a friend as a companion who was devout and austere as himself, he took up his abode on a small island not far from Genoa.

They spent the days and nights, allowing themselves as little sleep as possible, in prayer and penance, with roots and herbs for their only food. It is said that St Martin was nearly killed, on one occasion, by eating the root of a poisonous plant.

Whatever we may think nowadays of such a life, whether we consider it wise or foolish, we must always remember that the great object of St Martin, and men like St Martin, was to atone for their sins and glorify God by utter self-sacrifice.

The hermits did, and spoke, no evil. They were charitable. The spirits of pride and cruelty never entered their narrow cells. There are many, many true stories of their influence over the gentle creatures of nature, so often abused, so callously robbed of their innocent lives by heartless men.

Tender, anxious mother-birds would bring their young ones to the caves of hermits to share their crumbs of bread; little, delicate animals – like little squirrels, soft-eyed and swift-footed – would run to meet them without fear. Even wild beasts would do them no harm.

In some of the old pictures of St Martin you will see a hare painted at his feet. That is in remembrance of one of his miracles of mercy. He is said to have rescued the poor creature with a word, restoring it to fleetness, strength, and beauty, when it had been nearly torn to pieces by the dogs of cruel hunters.

On hearing that St Hilary was returning to Poitiers, St Martin followed him. His hope and desire was to continue the life of a hermit at some place within reach of his dear friend.

Eleven years passed away. Eleven long years of frequent fasting, prayer, and strenuous work, for St Martin made many converts. It is believed that he founded, during this time, the first monastery in France.

Then he was chosen Bishop of Tours, but his life was slightly clouded by the death of his beloved St Hilary. I say only 'slightly clouded', for St Martin could not really grieve that his friend should be numbered among those happy souls who have passed to their heavenly rest.

SAINT MARTIN OF TOURS

It was not long before the hermit of so many years found it impossible to stay in the busy city of Tours. But he could not give up the duties of his office. He chose a desert place, a few miles away, on high and rocky ground over the river, and went to live there, with eighty of his monks.

Once again it was in his power to practise the old austerities. He dwelt in a bare wooden hut, while many of his companions lived among the rocks.

St Martin was still the Bishop of Tours. So he could not follow his bent entirely as in the past. For this reason, doubtless, he became a missionary to the country people in western France.

The dauntless spirit of the soldier revived in his breast; he travelled far and wide, destroying heathen temples, preaching with fiery enthusiasm – resistless, passionate, inspired by God.

There is one particular incident in his career that gives a thrilling picture of the man and his times.

The haughty emperor who ruled the country refused, for some unknown reason, to see the Bishop of Tours who came to him on urgent Church affairs.

St Martin stood outside the palace, fasting, for seven days! Seven days without touching food, without sleep; seven days of waiting, to the scornful wonder of soldiers and courtiers; seven days in silence and patience!

Then the carelessness of the guards gave him an opportunity to enter. He strode into the presence of the emperor himself, surrounded by all his court.

Think of it!

There was the gaunt, pale figure of St Martin in his rough garb of camel's hair facing the gorgeous crowd. The emperor sprang to his feet. Shouts of anger and surprise burst from the lips of his people, swords were drawn, men leapt forward to seize the haggard monk, but at the first words he spoke – when his thrilling voice rang out – silence fell upon the throng.

Then they knew it was the dauntless Bishop of Tours, and hung upon his words. He did not plead in vain. All his wishes were granted, and the emperor loaded him with gifts.

When next he visited the court, after long persuasion, it is said that the empress herself prepared the meal for her royal husband and his honoured guest, serving them with her own hands.

While they were at supper, the emperor, to show honour to the bishop, offered him his own cup before he drank. A poor priest happened to be standing behind their chairs. St Martin accepted the cup, but turned and gave it to him. He meant, not so much to show his own humility, but to let the emperor see that the most humble servant of the Church should be reverently served before the most powerful earthly king.

SAINT MARTIN OF TOURS

There is a proof of St Martin's greatness that we should never forget.

It was an age of many cruelties. Men seemed quite indifferent to others' sufferings. A deed – a word – a thought of mercy shines out like a star in such a night of darkness.

Some heretics were condemned to death by the emperor. It was a blind and wicked sentence, for the pure cause of Christianity has never yet been well served by scorning the words of our Saviour: 'Blessèd are the merciful'.

There were two holy churchmen who, to their eternal honour, raised their voices in earnest protest. One was the good St Ambrose of Milan – you read his life in the last chapter – and the other was the valiant St Martin of Tours.

Our saint held his bishopric for thirty years. When he died, at the great age of eighty years, his people mourned him deeply.

He breathed his last at a place far distant from Tours, but his body was taken back to the city. Multitudes flocked out to meet the sad procession.

There is a beautiful legend that the barge which carried the holy dead along the river floated upstream without oars or sails, slowly and smoothly, to the sound of heavenly music in the wind. It was in the month of

November, when the year has grown old, but the trees on either bank burst into leaf and blossom as the boat passed them by.

It must have been on such a day as we enjoy in England, now and again, and still call by the name of St Martin's Summer, when the sky is blue and the air is warm for a brief season, as if the summer were indeed lingering with us still.

The festival of St Martin is celebrated on November 11th, and, as in the case of St Ambrose, the goose that is typical of the beginning of winter is often drawn as his emblem. Sometimes the old artists show a vanquished demon at his feet, and he is usually dressed as a soldier, in memory of his vision of the torn cloak.

He has always been a favourite saint in England. There are two churches, of the great number dedicated to his name, that we should hold in our affections more than all the rest.

The first is that little ancient building that crowns the hill overlooking Canterbury. Do you know that a Christian church has stood upon the same spot for more than fourteen hundred years, called by the name of the famous Bishop of Tours?

The second is a grand building in London, St Martin-in-the-Fields. In very old days it was known as St Martin-nigh-the-Cross, at the village of Charing. Today we call that village Charing Cross, but I do not suppose you know that *char* is a Saxon word meaning 'to turn', for the River Thames makes a great bend at this part. By the way, round about St Martin's Lane, near Charing Cross, there are lamp-posts – now used for electric lighting – on which you can see a tablet of St Martin. There he is, to this day, giving his cloak to the beggar.

It is long since St Martin's church stood 'in the fields', but it has lost none of the beauty of its graceful spire against the sky, though far and near the noise and stir of a great city beats against its quiet walls, like the waves of a restless sea.

So the character of the saint whom it commemorates, in spite of all the changes of time, remains with us still as an inspiration and example of courage and holiness.

SAINT AUGUSTINE OF HIPPO

Fourth–Fifth Centuries
Festival ⸺ August 28th

Justice shall walk before him:
And shall set his steps in the way.
— Psalm 84:14

It chanced on a fair summer day that a wise man was walking alone on the seashore.

The sun sparkled on the ocean and yellow sands. Now and again a seagull flew across the sky, or swept downward to the waves. Soft, fleecy little clouds were floating beneath the blue of heaven, and the whisper of the water was the only sound.

It was such a day as you have often enjoyed during your summer holidays at the seaside.

The lonely man was thinking deeply on a subject that even he could not understand, although he was one of the most learnèd and wise of men. He was thinking of the acts of God and trying to look into their hidden meaning.

Suddenly he came across a little child, who had made a hole in the sand into which he was pouring water very diligently.

'What art thou doing, my boy?' asked the wise man.

The child did not show any surprise at the question, or even raise his head.

'I am going to empty the waters of the sea into this hole, my Father', he replied.

'That is impossible, little one!' exclaimed the wise man, with a smile.

Then the boy looked up into his face.

'It is not more impossible than that thou canst understand the divine nature of God!' he answered.

The holy man was struck by the truth of the simple words, and then he saw it was no earthly child who had thus rebuked him, but a radiant angel. His heart was humbled. He covered his eyes with his hands, praying to be forgiven for the pride of which he had been guilty.

When he lifted his head, after a few minutes, he found himself alone with the sea and sky.

I think that is a very beautiful legend of St Augustine.

We have reached a time, in our book of saints, when we meet with perhaps the most famous Father of the Church, that is to say, one of the greatest writers and thinkers on religion during the first centuries of Christianity.

There are two well-known saints bearing the same name in the history of the Church. The first,

SAINT AUGUSTINE OF HIPPO

St Augustine of Hippo, of whom we are speaking now, lived in this world three hundred years before the coming of the second, St Augustine of Canterbury, whose story you will read in a later chapter.

The 'Doctor of Grace', to call Augustine of Hippo by one of his many names, was born in a small town called Tagaste, in Numidia, a part of northern Africa.

His mother's name was Monica, and she also was a saint – St Monica of pious memory – and his father was called Patricius. Monica was a Christian, but her husband did not share her faith at the time when their son was a little boy.

In his early schooldays – when he used to pray childishly that he might not be thrashed for neglecting to learn his lessons – the young Augustine was a high-spirited, warm-hearted, clever, affectionate boy. He disliked Greek, but loved to study Latin. But in truth he seems to have loved, better than anything else, the sports and games in which he could win applause.

He blamed himself, in after years, more severely than any one else would dream of blaming him, for eagerly reading the story of the Trojan prince called Aeneas, although he found no pleasure, oddly enough, in Homer's tale of the siege of Troy. He cared little for such studies as arithmetic, but 'sweetly vain fables' delighted him.

During a bad illness, when he was a young boy,

Augustine began to think seriously about religion and wished to be baptised, for he had heard much of Christianity from his devoted mother, but it was not yet to be. He recovered quickly, and his father's influence, for Patricius was still an unbeliever, may have partly caused the delay.

It was decided that Augustine should study to become a professor of rhetoric, or public speaking, for he had a good voice and a winning manner. But he wasted much of his strength and the too short days of his youth with idle, and even wicked, companions, sharing in their foolish and selfish pleasures.

This was a great distress to his mother, who understood both his weaknesses of character and the unawakened earnestness and nobility of his loving heart better than any one else in the world. His father also, as far as he could, devoted himself to the improvement of his son, intending to send him to a school of public speaking as soon as he could afford the expense, and looking forward anxiously to his worldly success. But Patricius died when Augustine was only seventeen, leaving him to the sole care of St Monica.

Do you remember the life of St Ambrose, Bishop of Milan? There is a very touching story of how St Monica was greatly troubled by her son's lack of true faith. St Ambrose consoled her by wise and quiet words.

'Let your son alone for a while. Only pray to God for

him. In time, by reading and thinking, he will find out what is wrong and put it away from him'.

The loving mother could not be satisfied so easily. She cried bitterly, entreating the bishop to see her son and argue with him. At last the holy man sent her home with these words:

'Go thy ways and God be with thee! Believe me, it is not possible that the son of those tears should perish'.

This gentle speech, as she often told Augustine in after years, sounded in her ears like a voice from Heaven.

St Monica, while she was living through the unhappy time of her son's lack of faith, dreamed one night that she saw him in the midst of the sea, drowning, while she herself was standing in safety upon a strong plank.

You can well imagine how she suffered. Suddenly an angel appeared, and, for a minute, she forgot everything else in her wonder. He lifted his hand and pointed to the plank. Then she saw that her son was rescued and standing by her side.

Do you see the meaning of this dream? It is very simple. The time came when he stood beside her indeed, upheld in the storms and dangers of the world, which are even greater than those of the sea, by a faith in God as sincere and unchanging as her own.

For about nine years, from the age of nineteen, St Augustine taught rhetoric, but still wasted his time and thoughts with idle companions, feasting, drinking wine, and winning garlands in foolish revels. But he had the sense even then, it must be allowed, to reject the absurd offers of men calling themselves wizards who were ready to promise the young speaker perpetual success in return for big enough payments.

'Though the prize I wish to win were made of pure gold', said St Augustine, 'I would never stoop to capture it by unfair means'.

He was fortunate in some of his friends, chief among them being an old doctor, and a very good, prudent youth of his own age. One of his young companions died at about this time, not only causing Augustine much sorrow, but filling him with a miserable fear of death. He mourned for his friend bitterly, becoming so restless and depressed that he left his home and went to a city called Carthage, where it was hoped he would recover his old high spirits.

After a time it is true that he made other friends, being always frank and affectionate, but he was no longer happy. His heart, unknown to himself, was yearning for deeper love, more perfect friendship, than any he had ever known. He was turning – slowly, surely, with many a hard struggle – towards God.

There is no need to tell you of this great man's

many sorrows and trials. Some day you can read all about them, if you care to do so, in his book called *The Confessions*. There you will find he confesses, or talks about himself, with great frankness, hiding none of his secrets, never sparing his own weakness or folly, always remembering that God alone is perfect.

He was like a traveller on a long road who knows if he can only go on to his journey's end that there is a haven of rest and peace awaiting him. But alas! he is so often tempted to linger in the noisy houses by the wayside, or slothfully throw himself down to sleep.

It was when Augustine went to Milan, after living in Rome, that he met with the good St Ambrose. In his own words, addressed to God:

'To him was I unknowing led by Thee, that by him I might knowingly be led to Thee'.

St Ambrose treated the young man with great kindness. Augustine listened eagerly to his preaching, at first for the mere sweetness and charm of his sermons, but very soon for their sincerity and holiness. St Monica followed her son to Milan, where she too was deeply moved by the sermons of the bishop, Ambrose.

So the hour came at last, when St Augustine had the strength of mind to give up the selfish, thoughtless pleasures that had so long held him captive. He deeply, sadly repented the restless discontent and vanity of his youth.

The light of God, at first seen only dimly, grew stronger and more brilliant every day. He saw that while everything else in the world changed, He alone is unchangeable. Everything comes from Him and belongs to Him.

One day, perhaps the most wonderful day in his life, St Augustine was alone in the garden with a friend, named Alypius. Alypius understood him well and gave him a great sympathy.

St Augustine, thinking of his conversion and need of help, wept most bitterly, throwing himself down upon the ground under a fig tree. He prayed to God to forgive him and protect him, repeating to himself again and again – 'How long? How long?' He meant how long would it be before he was able to find a way to peace of mind, casting all his doubts behind.

Suddenly a young voice from a neighbouring house – he never knew whence it came – began to sing these two words, softly, repeating them many times:

'Take, read; take, read'.

At first he thought it was some childish game, but he could not remember having heard them before. Then an idea flashed into his brain. He rose, went to the place where Alypius was sitting, and took up the Bible he had been reading before his tears had blinded him.

He seized upon it, and in silence read the first lines

upon which his eyes fell. It was one of the epistles, or letters, of St Paul, and the words he read touched him to the heart. They were so true! They swept away his doubts – they might have been written for him alone of all the world to read.

They told him the only way to please God and to find peace was to live a good life, giving up all wickedness, strife, and envy in the name of our Blessèd Saviour.

St Augustine showed the sentence to his friend Alypius, whose faith was also quickened as he read. Then they went into the house to St Monica. She had often grieved for her dear son in the past, but now her mourning was turned to joy, and they praised God together.

After this real conversion of his life and thoughts to holiness, St Augustine determined to give up his work as a professor of rhetoric. He prepared for baptism – you remember that his desire to be baptised when he was a boy had not been fulfilled – being joined by Alypius, his companion in the garden on the day of his awakening, and another dear friend.

He lived a quiet, serious life for some time, greatly rejoicing in the study of the Psalms and helpful discussions with several of his friends who had become Christians.

The great sorrow of his noble mother's illness and

death moved St Augustine, not to the expression of wild grief, but to calm resignation and loving remembrance of all he owed to her.

He describes, in one of the chapters of his *Confessions*, a long, last talk that he held with her, when they were alone together sitting at a window where there was a view of the garden, away from the noise of the streets.

It is a wonderful thing – is it not? – that the earnest, private talk of this mother and son, touching a depth and reaching a height of thought and feeling that very, very few of us can even imagine, should have been kept and read, again and again, for over a thousand years.

How the world has changed since they talked, and loved each other so well, in that peaceful room in their house on the River Tiber! Great cities have come and gone. Terrible battles have been lost and won. Famous men have lived and died. Countless books have been written, and printed, and forgotten. But the record of that hour's conversation of our saint with his pious mother remains as fresh and fragrant in its faith today as it was when they prayed and rejoiced together.

Five days afterwards St Monica became ill and quietly passed away, consoling her Augustine and a younger brother with hopeful and holy words. He must have been truly grateful to know that he had never spoken any harsh or unkind word to her. He had been worthy of her great devotion, and she often thanked God she had lived to see him a true Christian.

St Augustine was then in his thirty-third year. He wrote little more of his personal affairs after his mother's death, but his other writings, on the subject of religion and the Church, were very numerous.

He returned to his old home, Tagaste, and founded a community, or fellowship, of Christian friends for the sake of study and self-improvement.

After great hesitation, for he never ceased to regret the follies of his youth, St Augustine became a priest, and lived to be one of the greatest of teachers and preachers.

In the course of time he was made the Bishop of Hippo, and lived to a grand old age. His energy never flagged, for he laboured faithfully and earnestly to the end.

So you see that this far-famed Father of the Church was a true saint and a great champion of Christianity.

You will find out when you are older, and have read many books, that St Augustine is able to help us all by his perfect love of God, his knowledge of our natures, and his power of putting into words the thoughts, hopes, and feelings that stir our hearts in the most serious hours of life.

ST BRIDE

SAINT BRIDE

Sixth Century
Festival ⚘ February 1st

Bride, the queen, she loved not the world;
She floated on the waves of the world
As the sea-bird floats upon the billow.
Such sleep she slept as the mother sleeps,
In the far land of her captivity,
Mourning for her child at home.
     — St Bride's Hymn

IN a wild and beautiful country, where the grass is a more vivid green and the flowers are of brighter hue than in any other island in the grey seas, a great man was preaching the word of God. It was the fifth century – four hundred years after the birth of our Saviour – when the people of this lovely isle were very brave, but quite unlearnèd, and ruled by many kings.

The inspired man who preached to them in their own strange tongue, although he came from another land, awakened a quick response in their passionate natures. The story that he told of the perfect Child and His Holy Mother, His wondrous life of love and sacrifice, filled the people with great amazement and rapture.

They gathered round him when he ceased, questioning, talking among themselves, touching his hands and garments, anxiously studying his eager face.

There were many children in the crowd, held in their mothers' arms, or clinging to the hands of older brothers and sisters, who did not understand the reason of the scene, and cried aloud, some in fear, some in excitement.

One little girl, with wild-rose cheeks and glorious golden hair, did neither the one thing nor the other. She stood perfectly still, her hands locked together, her eyes shining like stars; her lips were parted by the swift, light breath of a heart that was fluttering like a bird set free from a cage; her little form was drawn to its full height on her strong, delicate bare feet; her whole being was a-quiver with heavenly joy.

The little girl, of all the throng, understood the great preacher best. She felt as a child feels who is very thirsty on a summer day and drinks a cup of cold, sparkling, pure water. She was so happy, so refreshed, so grateful!

From that hour – that minute – she became a child of God, loving His goodness, thinking of His beauty, praying for His mercy, following His truth.

Then the little girl went to the holy man who had preached to the people, and talked to him without fear or hesitation. He did not thrust her on one side, small as she was, for he saw that she was a spirited and noble child, blessed with many gifts, touched with holy fire, very steadfast for all her humility, very brave for all her gentleness.

The name of this holy man was St Patrick. The wild and lovely country where they met was Ireland. The little girl is known to us all as St Bride, or St Bridget.

After that eventful meeting with the patron saint of 'the Isle of Saints and Scholars' – as Ireland has been called – the young girl returned to the house of her father, who was a nobleman of Ulster, named Dubtach, and proved her devotion to our Saviour by making herself a little mirror to reflect His goodness.

She was so sweet and lovable, so rare and bright, that it hardly surprises us to hear that an angel had been her playfellow when she was a tiny child, helping her to make a little altar to God by lifting a stone too heavy for her small arms. In her own words: 'When I was a little girl I made an altar in honour of my God, yet with childish intention. Then an angel of the Almighty, in my presence, made holes in the stone at its four corners and placed therein four wooden feet'.

St Bride had to work in her father's house, but I am afraid it would not be wise for little housekeepers in general to follow her example, for she gave away the food of the family to any stranger at the gate who asked for it. It is said that other food was always found in its stead – her faith was so absolute in the kindness of our Father – but it is better for you, when your mother trusts you with household affairs, to obey her strictly and not give away her property.

St Bride was so generous and pitiful that she could never say 'No'. Once her father took her to the king's court, having told her – I hope it was only a jest of his – that he meant to sell her to the king because she was such an extravagant little daughter.

A beggar came along the road while the Lord Dubtach was in the house, and begged of St Bride waiting in the chariot outside. Having no money or possessions of her own, she gave him her father's sword, which had been a gift from the king. When Dubtach returned he was accompanied by His Majesty, and she frankly told them what she had done. Dubtach was very angry and the king amazed.

'I cannot refuse the poor!' cried the little girl; 'I would give away my dear father himself – and thou too, my king – if a beggar asked me'.

'Then I cannot buy her, Dubtach. She holds us both too cheap!' laughed the king.

So the Lord Dubtach took his daughter home again.

A few years afterwards a young nobleman begged to become her betrothed, for she had grown into the most lovely maiden in Ireland. But St Bride did not wish to marry. She had made up her mind to devote her whole life to God.

Her father tried to persuade her to accept the young man, and St Bride, dreading that he would force her to consent, prayed that her beauty might disappear; and it is said that her prayer was answered – but only for a little while.

With three other young girls St Bride stole away from her father's house to a place called the Hill of Uisneach, in the county of Westmeath, where a holy bishop, named Maccaille, having heard her story and questioned her very carefully, allowed her to become a nun, although she was not fifteen summers old.

Then a wonderful thing happened. It is called a miracle.

As St Bride knelt before the altar, having promised to give herself wholly to the service of our Lord, she became more beautiful than ever before; the bishop saw a flame of fire shining over her head, and, when she bent to kiss the dry wood at the foot of the altar, it grew green and living in token of her purity and holiness. It is because of this marvellous flame that she is called 'the Fiery Dart'.

St Bride's dress, or habit, was snowy white, and all the women who afterwards joined her – thousands of girls and women – wore the same, and joyfully obeyed the rules she made.

She built her own cell under a giant oak tree in a part of Ireland that has been called Kildare ever since, for the old word was *Cill-Dara,* meaning the Cell of the Oak.

In time a great number of people, both men and women, gathered round her, eager to follow her example of a life of prayer and worship and charity.

But you must not think that St Bride never left her cell. She travelled all over the country, honoured and welcomed wherever her fair face was seen and her gentle foot trod the earth.

She helped and blessed the poor. She was the counsellor and friend of kings. They say she had a school for metalwork at her own Kildare, and she loved music. Perhaps she often sang the great St Patrick's Hymn:

> I bind to myself today
> The Power of God to guide me,
> The Might of God to uphold me,
> The Wisdom of God to teach me,
> The Eye of God to watch over me,
> The Ear of God to hear me,
> The Word of God to give me speech,
> The Hand of God to protect me...
> The Shield of God to shelter me,
> The Host of God to defend me.

SAINT BRIDE

She was called by some 'the Mary of the Irish', because of the dream of a pious old man wherein he had looked upon the Mother of our Lord, whose radiant face resembled the face of St Bride.

Another of her fond names is 'the Milkmaid of the Smooth, White Palms', for she took an interest in the pastures and cows, so that milk, as well as fire, became known as her symbol.

She would play shepherdess at times, and once she was caught in a heavy rainstorm and returned to her home wet through. What do you think she did? Mistook a sunbeam gleaming across the room for a clothes-line, and hung her dripping white cloak upon it!

One of her nuns, towards the evening, came to tell her that the cloak was still there, so St Bride ran to get it and release the sunbeam, which slipped away after the sun.

Here is another story of the sweet St Bride.

One of her nuns, Sister Dara, was blind. They were talking so happily together on a summer day that they both forgot the passing of time. All their discourse was of the peace of Heaven and the perfections of God.

The sun set, the night passed, and as dawn crept over Wicklow Mountains her sight was restored to Sister Dara. She saw the pearly sky and the line of everlasting hills.

'Dear Mother', she said to her companion, after a little while, 'I wish I were blind again, for God's beauty is not seen so clearly when the beauty of the world is seen by the eyes'.

St Bride laid a soft hand on her forehead, and prayed; then she gently touched Sister Dara's eyelids, and her sight was gone once more.

Yet another story is of a poor man who had slain, unknowingly, a wolf that belonged to the king, and he was condemned to death. Directly St Bride heard of it she determined to see the king and beg his mercy. So she prayed for God's guidance and help, and set out for the court.

On her way to the court a wild wolf sprang into her chariot and allowed her to caress it. When they reached the king's house she calmly led the wild wolf into his presence.

'Here is a wolf in place of thine', she said; 'I know it will stay with thee at my bidding'.

The king was delighted at her gift; the wolf licked her feet and then crouched obediently before his new master, and the poor prisoner was set at liberty.

Wherever St Bride went she won the love of the people. Years after her life in this world she was remembered and honoured, not only by the Irish, but by the fierce Picts, the British, the Angles.

Many churches were raised to her memory. Do you

know that one of the most beautiful churches in the busiest part of London is dedicated to St Bride? It was built by a famous English architect, Sir Christopher Wren, in Fleet Street, where it stands to this day, a noble tribute to 'the Fiery Dart'.

St Bride passed away from this world at her own 'Cell by the Oak', surrounded by those who loved her. Her devoted nuns kept a fire burning, day and night, for many years, so their convent was known as the House of Fire.

Her own green island has never forgotten her. Even the dandelion is called 'the little notched flower of Bride', and the linnet is 'the little bird of Bride'.

The mothers of tiny babies appeal for her blessing. The boys and girls call her the saint of spring.

SAINT GREGORY THE GREAT

Seventh Century
Festival ⚹ March 12th

Lives of great men all remind us
We can make our lives sublime,
And, departing, leave behind us
Footprints on the sands of time
— Henry Wadsworth Longfellow

THIS is the story of the life of Pope St Gregory the Great. He was a holy man, a famous man, a powerful man. Many books have been written about St Gregory. Hundreds of his letters have been kept, for he wrote to the princes and kings of other countries, as well as to the bishops and great men of his own. He always gave them good advice, for he believed that the first duty of every ruler is to study the needs of his people, helping them to know the laws of God, and to lead happy, useful, free lives.

St Gregory was an Italian. He was born in the Eternal City, as Rome has been called.

His father and mother were able to give the boy a very good education, for they were not only rich people but belonged to an old and noble family, and wished him to be worthy of his name – brave, learnèd, truthful, courteous. He was a Christian, and thought deeply on the subject of religion before his own family had any idea of his ever belonging to the Church.

St Gregory studied law. He was quick of wit, clear in thought, earnest in effort; in brief, he was able to concentrate his mind. That means to give his whole attention to any work, or any subject, that he came across. Whatever he did, it was done with all his might. He never did anything by halves. His whole heart was in his work, as his whole faith was in God.

St Gregory was raised to a high office in Rome. He became the chief magistrate of the city, so he was like a judge, having to settle quarrels, listen to the stories of people who had been robbed or hurt, and order the punishment of the prisoners if they were found to have done wrong.

He was trusted and liked for his fairness by all who appeared in his court, although it was said that his words at times were sharp and biting.

The death of his father seems to have made a great difference in St Gregory's life. He was not only at liberty to do as he pleased, but became the owner of great wealth.

There was an order of monks in Rome which had been founded by St Benedict, and they were called

Benedictines. They lived an austere life – I told you in another chapter that austere means harsh or stern – and when St Gregory joined them it was with the intention of giving up all his time to heavenly thoughts, in strict obedience to their rules.

His willingness to serve his masters, submitting to their will without a murmur of complaint, helped him to govern others in the time to come. It taught him the great lesson of self-control.

After a time St Gregory became a priest. Then he left his fellow monks, unwillingly enough, at the command of Pope Pelgaius, who sent him on a long journey to the city of Constantinople. St Gregory took with him several of his brothers, for the sake of talking with them on the subject of religion. He began to write, at this time, one of his longest books, in no less than thirty-five volumes, that was not finished for many years.

After settling the business on which he had been sent to Constantinople, St Gregory returned to Rome. Then, for six years, he was abbot of St Andrew's, a monastery he had himself founded, but much of his time was spent with the pope, whom he advised and helped in many ways.

It was during these six years, which were among the happiest years of his life, that one of the greatest events in his history came to pass.

It is a simple story to tell, but you know some of the most surprising and important things in the world have started in a simple, quiet way.

One morning when St Gregory was walking through the forum, or public marketplace at Rome, he saw a group of beautiful boys, who were to be sold as slaves.

He stopped, looking with admiration and pity at their white skins, blue eyes, and fair hair.

'Are these youths pagan or Christian?' asked St Gregory.

He was told they were pagan.

'What is the name of the land from whence they come?'

'They are called English or Angles', was the answer.

'Not Angles, but angels!' exclaimed St Gregory. He asked the name of their king and many other questions.

'They shall be called to the mercy of Christ', he said.

Then he went on, deep in thought.

Long afterwards, as you will hear in the life of St Augustine of Canterbury, St Gregory the Great remembered the young Angles, with their angel faces, whom he had seen in the marketplace. That is why he is called the 'Apostle of England'. It was he who sent the first missionaries into this country, with the good tidings of our Lord Jesus Christ.

St Gregory, when the plague broke out in Rome,

was one of the first to offer his help. There were many deaths, but he worked among the sick without fear. To his sorrow, the pope, whose friend he had been so long, fell a victim to the terrible disease.

The city was filled with trouble and misery, but there was a feeling of great relief, even joy in the midst of sorrow, when the dearly beloved Gregory was chosen to be the new pope.

There was only one man who did not share in the general delight, the man whom it most concerned, the man who knew the difficulties and the dangers of power. And that was St Gregory. But he fled from Rome for another reason.

Yes, he fled from Rome! It was because he did not feel worthy of the honour. He was too humble to rely on his great gifts. As I told you, he had gladly learned to obey, but he did not wish to command.

He was quickly followed and found. In three days the people brought him back to the city in triumph, and he lived to be known as a Father of the Church and a truly great pope.

Faithful to the rules of the Order of St Benedict, which he had joined in his youth, St Gregory always wore the rough habit of a monk; he cared nothing for wealth or grand show, and he chose, on becoming the head of the Church, the beautiful title: 'Servant of the Servants of God'.

The new pope was a man of great gifts and a born leader. We know that he had thought much of the peoples in distant lands, especially of those lovely, fair-haired boys called Angles, to whom he had himself wished to preach the word of Christ. Now he sent missionaries far and wide.

English-speaking people owe even more to him than to St Augustine of Canterbury. It was his determination and zeal that inspired and upheld lesser men. He encouraged, rebuked, praised, urged them on. He was like a general on the battlefield, ready to face any danger himself and expecting the same of others, unmoved by ill fortune, seeing only one end to war – victory for the cause of right.

You must remember St Gregory served in the army of Christ, no earthly king, and our Saviour's soldiers must be merciful and true, without hate or anger.

St Gregory was pope for about fourteen years. He worked harder than he had ever worked before.

Quarrels in the city, attacks from enemies of Rome, disbelief and troubles among his brothers in the Church – St Gregory was able to deal with them all, for he was just, honest, and not afraid of any one in the world.

He did not allow the Jews, or other people who were not Christians, to be ill-treated. He tried to get rid of slavery. His power grew with the years. He could make war or peace as he judged best. He calmly resisted and mastered unjust kings and emperors.

St Gregory, in spite of the labours of his busy days, found time for the delights of art. He founded a school for sacred music, and the beautiful and solemn chants, called 'Gregorian' after his name and still used in Christian churches, were composed by him.

He was the constant patron of painting and sculpture. One of the greatest artists who has ever lived, named Michaelangelo, made a statue of this far-famed Father of the Church which perhaps you will some day see in Italy.

In all the old paintings he is shown in his robes as pope. His emblems are a book and pen. Sometimes he is seen, like St Augustine of Hippo, with a dove; sometimes he holds the small model of a church; sometimes an angel stands beside him with a raised sword. There are often a few sheets of music at his feet to remind people of his improvement in the music of the Church.

St Gregory did not live to be very old. He worked to the last, and ended his life of love and labour in this world at the age of sixty-four years.

He was buried in the church of St Peter, in the Vatican. The Vatican is the great palace of the bishops, or popes, of Rome.

St Gregory has been called 'the everlasting honour of the Benedictine Order', that is to say, the monks whom he joined as a young man were rightly proud of their holy, just, and learnèd brother.

He was a man of power, and he always tried to use it in the right way. In brief, he was a great man, a great ruler, a great Christian.

Now, I want to tell you two of the many legends of St Gregory.

In his youth, long before he became famous, a poor shipwrecked sailor begged for his help to return to a distant home.

St Gregory was poor himself, for it was just after he had given away his wealth and decided to live in poverty for the love of our Lord. All he had to give the sailor was a silver cup. So he put it in his hand with a word of blessing, and they parted.

Years afterwards, St Gregory became pope, as you know. Twelve important guests were invited to one of his first feasts; but on sitting down he saw, to his surprise, there were thirteen round the table. It was easy to find out the stranger. He was unknown to the host or the other men.

St Gregory drew him aside and asked his name. No doubt they looked at each other earnestly, but St Gregory did not remember him.

'I am the poor shipwrecked sailor to whom thou gavest thy last silver cup', said the unknown guest. 'My name is wonderful, and for my sake God will refuse thee nothing thou askest of Him'.

The second story is even more astonishing.

One day when St Gregory was in church, at the beginning of holy Mass, he happened to glance over the rows of people near him.

All his mind had been full of the words he had been speaking, but he felt a strange, sudden change of feeling. It was like a shock, as if he had been given a blow, and the only cause was the look on the face of an unknown man in the congregation – a look of unhappy doubt, even of scorn.

Their eyes met, and St Gregory was able to read his thoughts. He saw that the poor man did not understand, or believe, the word of Christ, although he longed for faith. He may have been a hard, cruel man. He may have been listening to the foolish, mean people who laugh at good and lovely things.

At first St Gregory prayed for his soul. He felt so sad. At the same time he knew that if it were the will of God the man's heart could be changed in a minute.

So then he began to pray for help to show him the truth of Christianity, that the man could see with his own eyes, or hear with his own ears, the grace of our Lord Jesus Christ.

A soft, golden light spread over the altar, like sunshine after rain. In the midst of it there stood the divine form of the Saviour of the world, but only two men in the crowded church were able to see the perfect vision.

One was the man of little faith, and the other was the saint who had pitied and prayed for him.

SAINT AUGUSTINE OF CANTERBURY

Seventh Century
Festival ✢ May 26th

As cold water to a thirsty soul,
So are good tidings from a far country.
– Proverbs 25:25

THE first Archbishop of Canterbury, our own Augustine, was a dear friend of St Gregory, whose life you have read in the chapter before this.

They may have been boys together – we do not know – but as men they worked, hoped, knew, and loved each other well.

St Gregory had more power than St Augustine; he was a man of greater character and strength. Again, the namesake of our archbishop, St Augustine of Hippo, held a place in the Church, and still holds it through his books, that St Augustine of Canterbury never reached.

I think that English children will like him more than the others, because the best years of his life were passed in England. He seems to belong to us. It was he who taught the fair Angles – angels, as you will remember St Gregory called them – to love and trust our Saviour.

As you know by the life of St Alban, there were Christians in Britain long before the coming of St Augustine, but the ancient Christian church was very different from the church that he founded.

Now, there was a strong king, named Ethelbert, ruling in Kent. His people were called the Jutes, and had had many battles with the powerful Saxons of Middlesex and Essex and the English of East Anglia.

King Ethelbert wished to be friends with the people of Gaul – you know that Gaul was the old name for France – so he asked the King of Paris for the hand of his daughter, Bercta, that their marriage might draw the two countries together.

Bercta was a lovely princess, very good, gentle, and pious. She was a Christian. King Ethelbert was a pagan. He worshipped the old, fierce gods of the past.

The French king accepted his offer. The princess consented, because she wished to obey her father, and also believed, having heard of the frank and honest nature of Ethelbert, that he would turn to her beautiful faith when he learned its truth.

So Bercta was sent to the court of the King of Kent, with noblemen and ladies to attend her, servants and soldiers for her protection, and rich gifts for her dowry. Most important of all, a Christian bishop was allowed to go with her.

She met and married the King of Kent in great happiness, for Ethelbert loved the fair girl for her sweetness and beauty, and she loved him for his courage and kindness.

The news of the wedding reached Italy. It was after St Gregory had become the Bishop of Rome. He had never forgotten his old wish that the people in that unknown island of Britain beyond the sea should become Christians.

When Bercta became the queen of King Ethelbert, this gave him the chance for which he had long waited.

It was impossible for Pope St Gregory himself to become a missionary; he had to choose another man. We can be sure that he prayed for help, and thought, deeply and earnestly, of different priests who might be worthy of so great a work.

At last his choice fell on an old companion of his own, a monk in his monastery of St Andrew, who held a high post there. His name was Augustine; he was a Roman, and not a very young man.

'This Augustine was very tall', says an ancient history of the monks of St Andrew. 'He was of a dark complexion; his face beautiful, but withal majestical'.

That is to say, he was a man of dignity, without pride, grave and kingly in look and bearing.

Some forty or fifty monks were chosen to go

with him. St Gregory saw them all, talked long with Augustine, gave them his blessing, and they set out on their journey.

It is very strange for us to hear, but the company of holy men were told the most surprising stories of the wild island of Britain. Whenever they halted, for prayer, or rest, or food, people gathered round, full of the dangers they would have to face, the men pitying them, and women in tears – everybody begging them not to go.

It is said that travellers tell strange tales; and it was just the same in those days as it is now. The few who had gone to Britain, and returned, spoke of the island people as 'barbarians', and that is a word meaning savage, rude, brutal men.

St Augustine was not afraid, but his brother monks became so unhappy and timid that he was obliged to listen to them.

'We shall be slain', they said; 'barbarians will never hear us. Let us return in peace'.

Their leader, very unwillingly, at last consented to go back and seek counsel, or ask the advice of St Gregory. So he turned his face once more towards Rome. His followers hoped the mission would be given up, but I think St Augustine went back only to please them. He was not the man to shrink from danger.

You will not be surprised to hear that St Gregory

bade them go on. He had the spirit of the early martyrs, and as his friend listened to his brave words his own courage revived. He wondered at himself. He felt the pride and glory of bearing the banner of the King of kings to a distant land.

The small company of Christians landed, after many hardships, in that part of England called Ebbsfleet, near the Isle of Thanet.

King Ethelbert met them on a chalky hill where today, looking across the stretches of far and fair country, we can see the dim tower of Canterbury Cathedral. With his courtiers and soldiers gathered round him, Ethelbert waited for the strangers from Rome.

St Augustine and his faithful monks slowly came towards him. They sang as they came a holy song, bearing before them a silver cross and 'the image of our Lord and Saviour painted on a board'.

It is a thrilling picture to treasure in our memories: the king, seated among his people, with the fresh winds blowing round them, the rustling of the trees, the song of the wild birds, the gleam of swords and the flutter of gay cloaks, the whisper of eager words, bending forward of heads, all eyes fixed on the little band of strange men – unarmed, unafraid – with the tall, majestic, dark-eyed Augustine at their head, and the sunlight glittering on the silver cross.

Then our saint began to preach, telling the king of

the life, the death, the resurrection of Jesus Christ, His miracles, His mercy, His promise of peace.

'I am the resurrection and the life: he that believeth in me, although he be dead, shall live: and every one that liveth, and believeth in me, shall not die for ever'.

Ethelbert listened in silence. This was the religion of his dear wife. This was the religion of the brave men before him – who had left their homes and crossed the stormy seas to save his people – this was the religion of perfect love.

When the king spoke at last, he spoke like an Englishman, justly and kindly, but with due caution.

'Thy words are fair', he said; 'but they are new to us and very strange'.

Then he promised the strangers to protect them, although he would not accept their faith so soon, and bade them go into the chief city of his kingdom, Canterbury, and dwell in peace there.

The band of monks marched into Canterbury, quietly singing the prayers of their Church:

'Turn from this city, O Lord, Thine anger and wrath, and turn it from Thy holy house, for we have sinned'.

Then, with a sudden burst of joy they cried:

'Alleluia! Alleluia! Give praise to God!'

The first Mass that the strangers from Rome held was under the roof of a little church named after the noble St Martin.

There were great changes in the country after the arrival of St Augustine, but they came slowly.

The Latin language began to be used, poetry was sung, pictures were painted, old and new laws were written down.

King Ethelbert, a year after listening to the first sermon preached on English soil, became a Christian. Then the men and women of Kent came in hundreds to be baptised.

Edwin, King of Northumbria, married a daughter of the Kentish king. One of St Augustine's followers, a fiery, earnest monk named Paulinus, was sent with the bride's party to the court of Northumbria to spread the faith in the north.

The power of Northumbria was so great that Edwin may be said to have ruled the whole of Britain. He was a good king, for it was a common saying in his day that 'a woman, with her baby in her arms, might walk unharmed from sea to sea'. No man would have tried to rob her or dared to treat her rudely in any way.

St Gregory the Great, when he sent St Augustine out as a missionary, had had the noble aim of joining together all the Christian churches in every land in love and brotherhood. It was with this object that St Augustine asked the bishops and priests of the old Christian faith in Britain to meet him. So they came together, but the exact spot has been forgotten. It was called the Synod of the Oak. The word 'synod' means a council, or meeting, of churchmen to talk upon religion.

Unhappily they could not agree, but St Augustine went on with his work in Kent. His home was always in Canterbury, but he travelled to other places. A cathedral was built in his time at Rochester and dedicated to St Andrew. Another was built in London and named after St Paul.

St Augustine never returned to Italy, but he went as far as France to be made a bishop. St Gregory wrote letters to him, and he wrote to St Gregory, with brotherly affection, to the end.

St Augustine died, less than a year after the famous Bishop of Rome had passed away, in the country he had made his own.

How the monks who had crossed the sea with him, any of the little band who were left, sorrowed for their friend and leader! What earnest prayers were said for him! What manly tears fell upon his grave! How the younger brothers must have crowded round the old men, listening to the story of that wonderful day when they met King Ethelbert of Kent, in the summer of long ago, when the silver cross and the picture of our Lord were uplifted in the fresh winds of Heaven and borne over English soil!

How the name of St Augustine must have passed from lip to lip, in praise, in love, in gratitude! God rest his soul, and may Britain never forget him!

ST ETHELDREDA

SAINT ETHELDREDA

Eighth Century
Festival ⚔ June 23rd

I looked far back into other years,
And lo! in bright array
I saw, as in a dream,
The forms of ages passed away.
— Henry Glasford Bell

ONCE upon a time – does that strike you as a peculiar way to begin the life of a saint? Perhaps it does, for we generally begin a fairy tale with those words. I think they occurred to me because I am going to tell you about a fair princess, who became a queen, and whose real adventures were as strange and interesting as the make-believe adventures of any maiden you have read about in a story book.

She lived a long time ago, three hundred years before William the Norman conquered England. That was in the year 1066, as you know, and St Etheldreda was born towards the end of 700.

This country was then under the rule of many different kings.

The King of East Anglia was called Ina, or Anna, and his wife's name was Hereswida. You will probably think that all these old kings and queens had rather difficult names to pronounce and remember. That is the truth, but it is interesting too.

Every name had its meaning. We are told that the common people knew our saint by a name we sometimes hear nowadays – Audrey. The choice of the common people – as it generally proves to be – was very sensible. 'Audrey' is a charming word.

The original spelling of Etheldreda was Æthelthrith. It is the woman's form of the man's name Ætheldryth, meaning 'noble troop'. She is also called Ethelred, but I think we will keep to the popular Etheldreda.

The king and queen of East Anglia had many children. The feeling in their house, in spite of the wars and other troubles of an unsettled country, was one of peace and good will. They must all have loved one another dearly, for their after lives show a sympathy and understanding that only come from happy childhood.

We can be certain, although it may not be found in any records of the time, that the daughters of the royal house were greatly influenced by the example and teaching of their mother's sister. She is one of the saints of the Church, St Hild, or Hilda, the famous abbess of Whitby.

There is one fact at least about St Hild that every

English child ought to know.

Her abbey, built on the dark, rugged cliffs overlooking the North Sea, was the school of some of the finest scholars and most saintly bishops and priests. She herself was an extraordinary woman, the friend and counsellor of churchmen and kings.

Her greatest glory, however, is that of having encouraged the genius of our first English poet, the inspired Cadmon.

Cadmon was only a cowherd, who knew nothing of the art of verse, for he could not even join in the poor attempts at songs that his companions invented at their rough merrymakings to chant to the harp.

On a certain night, as he was sleeping in a stable, One appeared to Cadmon who said, calling him by name:

'Sing, Cadmon, some song to Me!'

'I cannot sing', he answered.

'Thou canst to *Me*', said the voice.

'Tell me what to sing', cried the poor cowherd.

'Sing the beginning of all living things!'

So Cadmon sang his first poem, and, on the following day, he went to the abbess, Hild, and told her his dream.

She was deeply moved, for she considered that he had been directly inspired by Heaven, and bade him turn a passage from the Scriptures into verse. His success in doing this caused the abbess intense joy. She helped him to become a monk, for his sudden burst of song seemed, to the people of that day, to be simply divine.

'Others after him strove to compose religious poems, but none could vie with him, for he learned not the art of poetry from man, nor of men, but from God'.

Let us return to the story of Etheldreda.

Her childhood was spent very happily in the companionship of her brothers and sisters. Of the three elder girls, Sexburga was perhaps the most dearly loved by Etheldreda. Their lives were very much alike, as you will hear.

Ethelburga, the next sister, lived to become the abbess of Farmontier. Little is known of Erminilda. Withburga, the youngest sister, was the most austere of them all, for she became a recluse in Norfolk. A recluse is one who lives apart from others, entirely devoted to prayer, penance, and perpetual thoughts on religion.

St Etheldreda was still very young when her father wished her to marry. Doubtless there were many princes and nobles anxious to win the lovely daughters of the King of East Anglia. Sexburga had already become the wife of the King of Kent.

Etheldreda was very beautiful. She wore the handsomest dresses she could get and decked herself with jewels, being especially fond of twining strings of pearls round her slender throat.

The bridegroom chosen for her by her family was named Tombert, ruler of a Saxon colony near her home.

We do not know whether at first she loved the man so chosen to be her husband. In truth, her mind and heart were already turning towards an ideal very different from the life of a grand lady. She often longed to be alone, away from all the courtiers, flatterers, and servants who surrounded her. Even her girl's vanity began to fall away, like a flimsy, outworn cloak.

She yearned, more and more every day, to follow the example of the saints. As they had given their lives to the continual worship of our Lord and honouring His Holy Mother, so this young princess was slowly realising that no lesser service would calm her soul. She was unhappy in the world, restless, dissatisfied, like a free bird of Heaven in a golden cage.

Her young husband, fortunately for Etheldreda, understood her growing piety. He did everything in his power to help her. A great sympathy and equally devout ideas made them kind and loving to each other. Only two or three years after their marriage, however, Tombert died.

Now, if she had been wiser, Etheldreda, who was still little more than a girl, would have taken the veil, that is, become a nun, directly after her husband's death. It is a mystery why she continued to live the busy life of a princess. But it was only in outward show, for all her thoughts were those of a strict recluse.

It is an even greater mystery how she ever was persuaded to consent to a second marriage. I expect it was the scheme of her father, for the youth he wished her to accept was Prince Egfrid, son and heir of Oswi of Northumbria, one of the most powerful Saxon kings.

Egfrid was kindly and well-meaning, but not a strong character. He resembled Tombert in his good will, but not in his unselfish piety.

At all events, Etheldreda consented to marry him, to the satisfaction of her people, and the ceremony took place in the presence of her father and many guests.

It was not long before the young princess became a queen. Her second husband, having succeeded to the throne of Northumbria, was no longer satisfied with Etheldreda's simple, severe way of living. She was more like a nun in a convent than the mistress of a big house.

He is not to be blamed for wishing her to act the part of a queen. Having married, even against the secret wishes of her heart, she ought to have tried to make him happy in his own way, for he certainly tried to please her. Perhaps she did so – who can tell? – for it was several years before she finally determined to take the veil, and not until her husband had solemnly given his consent.

So St Etheldreda threw away her handsome dresses, untwined the pearls from her beautiful throat, and laid the crown of a queen on the altar.

All would have been well if King Egfrid had not broken his word. He suddenly changed his mind and declared that his wife should return to the court, in spite of the solemn pledge he had given not to force her back.

Fearing the violence of his temper she fled from her convent with two attendants, who were very young girls, bearing the quaint names of Sewerra and Sewenna.

The angry king pursued her. Her fear was very great, for she knew her capture would mean captivity; not the captivity of an ordinary prisoner, but a return to the worldly life she had so joyfully resigned.

It was a wild and desolate country. St Etheldreda must have felt very helpless and lonely, but her heart did not fail her, for she believed that God would uphold her. She cheered the two little sisters, Sewerra and Sewenna, bidding them pray for her safety without ceasing.

At length they reached a high and rugged rock.

The king was close upon them. His anger had grown to fury. He lost all self-control and even broke his word by hotly denying that he had ever consented to his queen's departure.

St Etheldreda and her frightened companions climbed the steep rock with hurried feet – slipping, falling, stumbling on – with appealing voices raised to Heaven.

They heard the roar of the sea below them and the howling of the gusty wind. There was the mournful cry of storm-tossed birds, and they saw the jagged line of the cliff like a cloud resting on the earth.

Then the king and his followers came riding out of the shadows, cruelly spurring their tired horses. They saw the three figures of the women fluttering as it seemed on the side of the rock, near to its summit.

The king dropped from his saddle and rushed forward, but as he drew near, and nearer still, the tide of the sea came rolling in. The hungry waves swept over the sand and stones and curled round the base of the rock in widening, long, white curves.

St Etheldreda knelt upon the hard ground and prayed, with tears of gratitude streaming down her face. The little sisters clung to her, looking down from the dizzy height on the rising sea.

The king was baffled. What could he do? It was impossible to fight with the stormy waves. Every minute they leapt higher. He was obliged to fall back, and his waiting followers were unable to offer him sympathy or counsel.

They saw he was conquered by a power far greater

than that of any king. Soon the rock was entirely surrounded by water. No man would have dared to climb, for he could not have gained a footing on its rough sides, and the big waves would have swept him away.

Far into the night, when the troop of men had galloped away, St Etheldreda praised and thanked God. The weary maidens, Sewerra and Sewenna, fell asleep, nestling in the folds of her cloak.

As soon as the light of morning shone over the sea, stretching away at low tide in the distance, St Etheldreda aroused her young companions, and then slowly, with great difficulty, scrambled down the rock, astounded to remember how swiftly they had climbed on the previous night.

The rock has been called St Ebb's Head ever since.

By noon the three women were far on their journey. It was not until St Etheldreda had crossed a wide river – known to us now as the Humber – that she consented to rest. Then she struck her staff into the ground, said a prayer, and laid herself down to sleep. Sewerra and Sewenna sat beside her on either hand to keep guard.

Do you remember the miracle of the staff of St Christopher? It burst into leaf and flower in remembrance of his vision of the Holy Child. St Etheldreda dreamed a dream that reminds us of that beautiful legend.

She saw her staff grow into a stately tree, and she knew that her work would prosper and live after her. She interpreted, or read, her dream as a divine message from the One who had protected and saved her.

It is said that King Egfrid never troubled her again. Perhaps he regretted his broken word. Perhaps he had learned, on the night when the sea barred his way, that no man can oppose the will of God.

The Isle of Ely had been given to St Etheldreda by her father as a dowry. It was there that she ended her wanderings. No doubt the faithful Sewerra and Sewenna lived with her for the rest of their lives.

It was at Ely that St Etheldreda built her convent, with the help, it is supposed, of one of her brothers. She was followed thither by her dearest sister, Sexburga, who had married the King of Kent.

St Etheldreda's piety and many acts of devotion became known far and wide. Young girls were sent to be educated under her care. She does not seem to have possessed the power to be the ruler and counsellor of statesmen and priests, like her aunt, St Hild of Whitby, but her good influence as abbess of Ely was very great. She ruled well, strictly, justly, but with affection and understanding.

St Etheldreda did not live to be old. Bearing a long illness with patience and sweetness, she thanked Heaven for teaching her to suffer. Her throat was affected, and she often spoke of the time when, as a young princess, she had adorned it with pearls.

'In my vanity I would hang a necklace of worthless beads round my neck', she said, 'but it has pleased God to hang an affliction there instead. It is well!'

So she passed away, happy and devout, never so truly a beautiful queen as on the day that she died a humble nun.

The stately cathedral at Ely – changed as it has been through the centuries – is a lasting memorial of St Etheldreda.

The story of her life is told in the ancient sculpture at the top of the high pillars. There are many groups, showing all the chief events. We see her being married to her second husband, with her father, the King of East Anglia, giving her away; taking her religious vows, her crown laid upon the altar, with the Bishop of York blessing her, and an abbess placing the veil on her head; her escape from the violent rage of King Egfrid; her wonderful dream; her last illness; and, perhaps the most interesting of all, her second burial after her body had rested in the ordinary cemetery for years. She was believed by some of the people of that day to have been laid in a marble coffin made by angels.

St Etheldreda is represented, like all the other Saxon princesses who became saints, as very richly dressed.

She wears a golden tunic and golden shoes. Her flowing mantle is clasped over the black habit of the nun. She is crowned to show her rank. She holds a pastoral staff in one hand, a book in the other. She is also painted carrying a lily.

St Ethelwold, a writer of Winchester, who had a great veneration for her, has drawn her in his works. She appears as a very fair woman, holding a lily and wearing beautiful draperies.

If ever you go to Ely Cathedral, which is dedicated to St Peter and St Etheldreda, give a little thought to the lovely Saxon queen of twelve hundred years ago.

SAINT SWITHIN

Ninth Century
Festival ✦ July 15th

He prayeth best, who loveth best
All things both great and small;
For the dear God who loveth us,
He made and loveth all.
　　　　　　– Samuel Taylor Coleridge

How little we know of the good St Swithin! Ask your friends on July 15th to tell you why it is called St Swithin's Day. Ask them to tell you why, if it rains then, it is supposed to rain for forty days afterwards. Perhaps one out of the many will be able to give you some idea, but I am certain that the greater number will frankly admit they know nothing at all about it.

After all, it is an important matter. Too much rain spoils the summer holidays; too little is bad for the fields and gardens. It makes one wonder whether St Swithin has really anything to do with it. Ought we to blame him if there is a downpour on July 15th, and praise him if the sun shines brilliantly all day long?

Let us try to find out the origin – that means, you

know, the beginning, or event that was the first cause – of the idea of forty days' wet weather when it rains on St Swithin's.

First of all, we must take a long journey. It is not an ordinary journey over land or sea, but into the past. We must travel backwards, instead of forwards, that is the only difference.

We shall leave nearly everything we know behind us, for the time we have to study was before the House of Windsor, or the Stuarts, or the Tudors, or even the Plantagenets ruled over England. It was before the Normans conquered the Saxons. Our land was divided into many kingdoms. Wessex was governed by a strong king named Ethelwulf. His kingdom was threatened by constant attacks from a foreign people called the Danes.

The Danes plundered London and Canterbury, sweeping up the River Thames, but Ethelwulf was a great warrior and fought for his people stubbornly.

The Danes were not Christians, and the dread of the return of the worship of their fierce and strange gods, named Odin and Thor, aroused the priests to help the king with all their power. Among his most loyal and devoted counsellors was a certain Bishop of Winchester, who was named Swithhun, but is known to us now as St Swithin.

No wonder that he loved King Ethelwulf! They were friends of many years, for the bishop had been the king's guardian and tutor. It is very likely that Ethelwulf's determined resistance to the Danes was encouraged and sustained by the enthusiasm of St Swithin, who was a dauntless soldier of the Cross.

After long fighting, to the great relief of the people of Wessex, the Danes were driven away. For eight years there was a reign of blessèd peace.

Worn and weary with strife, King Ethelwulf was only too happy to lay down his arms. As the valiant leader of his men in war, he had won their affection and trust. They found him a good ruler. St Swithin was his chief minister.

We can well imagine that happy time. The plundering Danes from over the sea were gone. Fathers and sons were no longer called from their homes to battle. The great abbeys and humbler churches of the land were saved from ruin.

Now, the brave King Ethelwulf was the father of many sons – four sons were born to be kings of Wessex.

We cannot doubt that his old master, the Bishop of Winchester, had much to do with the training of the young princes. It may have been from his lips that the youngest and most promising of the boys learned the great truths that our Saviour taught.

It may have been that the wise St Swithin first inspired that boy to live so nobly that he fulfilled his own desire – written long, long afterwards – 'I have striven to live worthily, and to leave to the men that come after me a remembrance of me in good works'.

Although St Swithin did not see the young prince in his prime, we know that his heart would have been filled with joy and he would have thanked God for the virtue and glory of his deeds.

At the entrance of the city of Winchester, once the home of St Swithin, there is a grand statue of that fair-haired Saxon boy in his manhood. Do you know who he is? He bears the name of our noblest king, a man whom we honour more and more as the centuries go by; a man whom England will never forget – it is Alfred the Great.

Now, to begin at the beginning of St Swithin's life, he was sent to Winchester as a child. Educated in a monastery, he seems to have been intended by his parents for the Church. At all events, he made up his own mind to become a priest. He would have made a brave soldier, as the part he played in the war against the Danes in after years plainly shows. He would have made a good traveller, for he was indifferent to hardships and loved nature. But all his deepest thoughts, interests, and hopes were centred in the religious life.

He would have been quite content – more than content, very grateful – to have passed all his days as an unknown priest. His saintly spirit was really untouched by the troubles, the wars, the dangers through which

SAINT SWITHIN

he lived. He took his part as a duty in the affairs of the world. It was King Ethelwulf who made him Bishop of Winchester, his chief adviser and the friend of his sons; and the king's confidence was repaid a thousandfold.

At the same time St Swithin, as we can judge from the few, but very decided, facts we can read in old books, was a man of quiet, simple nature, without pride, disliking pomp and show.

He was fond of music; perhaps not as learnèd as some of his brethren, but with wisdom that is deeper than any book knowledge. Above everything else, he was a holy man, worshipping God in His works, seeing His splendour and beauty in the clouds, the earth, the sunshine, the wind, the storm.

We are told that St Swithin, when he was Bishop of Winchester, made his way to all parts of his diocese – that is to say, the different places it was his duty to rule. He must have known the country well and all the people, rich and poor.

Unlike the great St Hugh of Lincoln, whose story you will find in a later part of this book, St Swithin seems to have found a continual delight in the fields, the woods, and the wild flowers.

St Hugh rarely lifted his eyes from the ground, for all his thoughts were of the lasting beauty of the heavenly life. St Swithin looked at the fleeting beauty of this world.

Have you ever thought, as you wander down a country lane, of the way our English flowers tell us the story of old-time piety and virtue?

The common, small bindweed is the emblem of humility. The blue convolvulus means repose. The cowslip is pensiveness; the daisy, innocence; the dock, patience; the flowering reed, confidence in Heaven; the wild geranium, tranquillity; the snowdrop, hope.

Many of the wild flowers were dedicated to our Saviour's Blessèd Mother, as the marigold, or Mary's Gold, Our Lady's Mantle, and the Madonna lily. The red campion is Mary's rose, and the mullein with its tall spike of yellow blossoms was the Virgin Mary's Taper.

The saints were known by their flowers. Herb Christopher was named after the Christ-bearer. Sweet Basil belonged to St Basil, and Sweet Cecily to St Cecily. A Flower of Gold was the very old name for a lovely blossom, then it became known as the July Flower, then as the Gilliflower, and today we call it carnation.

There is a legend that the pansy – pansies, by the way, mean thoughts – was once as sweetly scented as the violet, but so many people looked for it in the fields, for the sake of its perfume, that the corn was trampled underfoot. So the good little flower prayed that its scent might be taken away, then it would be less desired, for loss of corn meant hunger for the poor. Its prayer was granted, as we know, for it has no perfume today.

Here is another sweet story for you before we leave off wandering among the flowers.

In Paradise, when the flowers were first made, there was a little pale, starry plant that was so small it could hardly be seen among the sedges at the waterside where it grew. It feared that the Lord would not remember to give it a name.

'Forget-me-not! Forget-me-not!' it whispered.

The herb-o'-grace was named, and the pale primrose, and the fiery gorse, and the daffodils 'that come before the swallow dares and take the winds of March with beauty'.

'Oh, forget-me-not! Forget-me-not!' sighed the little starry plant, unheeded.

Then the scarlet pimpernel was given its name, and the fragrant lavender, and the tinkling harebell.

'Forget-me-not! Forget-me-not!'

The Lord bent down and touched the pale starry plant.

'Thou alone', He said, 'hast not the faith to wait for Me, so thou shalt be called forget-me-not, but to show My remembrance of thee thou shalt be the colour of the heavens for evermore'.

So the forget-me-not was thrown down to the earth, where it can be seen all through the summer just the colour of the sky.

St Swithin was Bishop of Winchester for many years. He did not live long enough to see Alfred the Great ruling Wessex, for when Ethelwulf died, his eldest sons, one after the other, became kings. We are glad to know that the country was at peace during the last years of St Swithin. It was safe for him to ride, or tramp, along the roads and the lanes he knew so well.

It is pleasant for us, when we are in the country, to think of those far away times. There were very few houses, or carriages, or even travellers.

I think the gentle Bishop of Winchester would stroll along, or amble on his mule, without hurrying. The cool, fresh days of spring, the summer sunshine, the autumn winds, the winter rains, would all be welcomed in their turn by him.

He would listen to the bird calls, and watch the shadows of the trees on the road; he would notice the first buds to burst open; his quick eye would follow the dart of little bright-winged insects; he would know by the clouds when a storm was coming.

If a poor peasant passed him by, dusty and tired; or one of his own monks, with eyes bent on the ground; or a knight with his long sword at his side – the bishop would pause and give each one his blessing, and they would turn their heads to watch him out of sight, you may be sure, for even to look into his good face used to make them all feel better men.

It was found, when St Swithin had passed away from this earth to his heavenly home, that he did not wish his body to be buried in a place of honour.

Always holy and wise, he had never thought of himself as a king's minister or great bishop. He knew that the Master whom he served, and in whose footsteps he tried to walk, had been meek and lowly and loved the poor.

St Swithin begged, in his will, to be laid in a humble place, not a church, where the feet of wayfarers might tread upon the grass over his grave and the rain of Heaven might fall upon it.

His loving people obeyed him, but a hundred years afterwards there was a rich shrine put up in the cathedral church of Winchester. It was to hold the remains of our saint. I think it would have been better to leave his simple grave alone.

Now, you have heard the true life of the good St Swithin, but your question is still unanswered – why do people say that forty days of wet weather follow a shower of rain on St Swithin's?

Nobody is quite sure. We only know that he loved the rain as much as he loved the sunshine, for he knew, as we should all remember, that both alike are the priceless gifts of God.

ST DUNSTAN

SAINT DUNSTAN

Tenth Century
Festival ~ May 19th

No wrath of men, or rage of seas
Can shake a just man's purposes;
No threat of tyrants, or the grim
Visage of them, can alter him;
But what he doth at first intend,
That he holds firmly to the end.
— Robert Herrick

WITH the life of St Dunstan we have reached the tenth century of the Christian era, nine hundred years after our Lord lived upon earth.

This is the story of an Englishman, one of the strongest Englishmen in the history of our country before its conquest by William the Norman.

As I say, Dunstan was a strong man, so powerful in his own days that it is hard for us to read his true character. He made enemies, as the powerful always do. Many were jealous of him; many could not understand him; many feared him.

He was a saint, we know; but there have been stories told and written of his hardness and pride. It is better, before we believe them, to try to find out what was said of him by a man who spoke the truth and knew him well.

A life of St Dunstan was written, directly after his death, by one of his pupils, a priest whose name is unknown, for he simply calls himself 'B'. There we read of Dunstan as kind and gentle, pious as we know he must have been, and faithful to his friends.

I will tell you another little fact about him, only found out years and years after his time. He was an artist, as you will read later on, and one of the few drawings that has not been lost or destroyed is a sketch of a boy's head, just a few faint lines, with the words written underneath it in his own hand – think of it, written a thousand years ago! – 'Wulfrid, cild'. That means, as we write in these days, 'child Wulfrid'.

It was drawn when Dunstan was a middle-aged man, but it has been found out that he had had a little brother of that name, who died when our saint himself was very young. It shows us, that little sketch, the tender remembrance of the man in the midst of his many cares as the friend of kings. He must have loved the child Wulfrid. Poor child Wulfrid, long forgotten, but now remembered.

St Dunstan was born near Glastonbury. His father, named Heorstan, was a rich man, brother of two bishops, of Wales and Winchester. It is said that his mother was called the Lady Kynedritha.

When he was about nine years old he was sent to school; that is to say he lived in a monastery, with other boys, and studied the subjects that are taught in our schools now, but with a difference.

The monks, who were his masters, made him write and illuminate very carefully, without blots or faults, or any other signs of hurried work. To illuminate is a fine art, for it means to draw, paint, and form your capital letters with skill and beauty. Straight lines, curves, and circles must all be correctly made, flowers and leaves must be copied as perfectly as the hand can make them, the colours well chosen, the figures true to life.

If ever you have a chance to hold an old book, illuminated in the far past, in your own hands, be sure to treat it as delicately as if it would break at a touch, turn the leaves lightly, and never put even the tips of your fingers on a painting. Remember you are looking at the work of men who did it for the glory of God, and because they saw and loved the beauty of His smallest, as much as His greatest, gifts.

St Dunstan became an artist and musician, being able to make carvings, paint, and play the harp. He was a small, thin boy, with fair hair. He was fond of animals, and could win their affection and obedience so easily that his companions thought he used a charm to bewitch them. He sang songs and legends and old chants. Indeed, he loved music so well that he carried his harp about with him wherever he went.

There is a story that once, when he was alone in his cell after he had become a monk, this beloved harp was hanging on the wall untouched, for St Dunstan feared that it might draw his mind from holy thoughts. But an angel appeared, and played upon it the sweetest, softest music ever heard.

The monastery where St Dunstan went to school, at Glastonbury, was rich in books, for many scholars had lived there, or been its guests, and had left their works behind them. The boy studied and read so much that his health failed and he was very ill.

His fame as a student and musician had travelled far, even to the court of Athelstan, the king of the Saxons in Wessex.

So, when he was well again, St Dunstan was sent to the king, who treated him well and loved to hear him sing. The courtiers did not look upon the fair-haired, thoughtful youth so kindly. Even his own kinsmen were jealous. The foolish cry of 'sorcerer' was raised against him, for they said he used magic or wicked spells to win praise and affection.

He was driven from the king. A party of young men, cowards all, seized upon him one day when he was walking alone in a country place, and threw him into a shallow, muddy pond. It might have killed him, for he was not strong and they handled him with violence and cruelty.

He crept out of the water to find himself alone. He was covered with dirt, half choked, bruised, and shaken. Some dogs, from a farm near by, came running up and treated the poor boy more kindly than men. They stayed beside him, licked his hands and face and tried to comfort him, he said, 'by friendly wagging of their tails'.

After this adventure St Dunstan left the court, too unhappy to stay any longer, and went to live for a time with his uncle, the Bishop of Winchester.

Once more he fell dangerously ill. His recovery was long and tedious, but it seems to have given him time for serious thought. When he rose from his bed at last, and dragged himself into the healing sunshine, the frail youth looked upon the world with new eyes.

He was filled with the mercy of God and felt that his life had been spared for holy work. He would be a monk and give his whole heart to the worship of his Lord.

There is no doubt that St Dunstan's nature was very ardent. He was full of feeling, and he thought at this time that it was his duty to live the life of a hermit for the rest of his days.

So, after joining the order of monks called Benedictines, he made a little cell for himself, just high enough to stand upright and long enough to lie at full length, and lived there all alone.

He dreamed strange dreams and saw many holy visions, but he was not the man to remain a hermit. He was too bright and eager, too fond of work, music, the company of friends, books, and busy affairs.

There is a well-known legend of St Dunstan that must have been told in the first place to show his high, bold spirit. It is a comic old legend that perhaps will make you laugh.

The good saint was an artist, as I told you, not only a painter, but a skilful worker in metal.

One day, when his hands were busy with his tools, his little furnace was alight, and he was doing his best as all craftsmen should, the Evil One suddenly appeared.

He hoped to tempt St Dunstan away from his work, to make him idle and careless, so that he would forget to say his prayers or do his daily duty.

At first the Devil stood by the door, beckoning and smiling very pleasantly. St Dunstan took no notice, but quietly began to heat his pincers at the fire. So the Evil One stole in, nearer and nearer, speaking softly of the pleasures he had to offer. Never a word said the saint. At last the Devil stood at his elbow, whispering close to his ear.

The minute had come! What do you think St Dunstan did?

SAINT DUNSTAN

Snap! He seized the Wicked One by the nose with his red-hot pincers, and held on till he screamed and bellowed and howled and roared and yelled!

After a while St Dunstan left the hermit's cell behind him.

One of his best friends was an old lady, Ethelfleda, who was very pious and spent her great wealth in charity. He helped her, and enjoyed, in her company, the quiet, religious talk, the exchange of thought, the peace and holiness that he missed so much in the anxious, great affairs of his after life.

At the death of the Lady Ethelfleda, St Dunstan returned to court. King Edmund was then upon the throne.

The dreamy boy with his harp, whom the rough young courtiers had ill-used so shamefully, had grown into a strong, self-reliant man.

King Edmund liked him at first, but old enemies, even more jealous than in the days when his chief gift was the singing of sweet songs, tried to get rid of so dangerous a rival by persuading the king to treat him unkindly. They feared his keen eyes, love of truth, and pity for their slaves. St Dunstan hated slavery, and believed that every Englishman should be free.

He was about to leave the court for a second time, to return to books and quiet work, when something happened that altered the whole course of his life.

King Edmund was out hunting. A red deer, at the end of a long day's sport, crossed his path, and the king sped after it. His horse dashed over the ground at breakneck speed, but the deer outran him. The king's disappointment made him spur his steed to greater efforts. The deer leapt down the steep cliffs of Cheddar. Then the king tried to draw rein, for he knew it would be impossible to follow.

He thought that his end had come, and, in that wild minute, repented of his unkindness to Dunstan. The horse, as if an unseen hand had caught the bridle, was checked in his mad gallop at the very edge of the cliffs, and the king was saved.

He turned and rode back to the court, without a word to his frightened followers. Dunstan was called out. The king bade the servants bring another horse and told our saint to mount and ride with him. Dunstan obeyed, wondering a little, but without fear or hesitation.

The royal train swept over the marshes to his home. The king, when they reached the cathedral, gave him the kiss of peace and turned to the throng behind them.

'Behold!' he said, 'this is the abbot of Glastonbury!'

So St Dunstan became an abbot. From that day to the end of his life he served the Church and his country faithfully, religiously, and boldly.

SAINT DUNSTAN

St Dunstan became King Edmund's chief minister. It was seen at once that he was the man to save the kingdom from its foes at home and abroad.

The first thing he did was to gain the friendship of the king of the Scots, who helped him to fight and drive away the Danes. So the kingdom of Northumbria came under the rule of Edmund, but the king was slain by a robber soon afterwards, and his brother Edred came to the throne.

St Dunstan had now reached the highest place in the country. His word was law. We know little of the new king, for he reigned a very short time, and Edwig succeeded him.

If you want to understand St Dunstan's public work you must read, some day, the full history of England at that time. Do you know what it means to be a great statesman? A statesman is one who is able to look ahead, to understand the needs of the people, to protect their rights, to think of the good of all, and to uphold the honour and safety of his country.

St Dunstan was a great statesman. His first care was the kingdom he ruled, but he had no dislike of other peoples, for he studied them and treated them fairly – even his old foes, the Danes, were free to do as they chose in their own part of the country. I need not tell you that many of the rich and powerful lords in Wessex were angry with St Dunstan for the very reason that should have made them honour him – his justice and courage.

King Edwig was a weak, foolish youth. He had married a young girl as weak and foolish as himself. They were really fond of each other. That is the only good word to be said for either of them.

Edwig, in the middle of the feast after he was crowned, left the dining hall to talk and jest with his wife in their private rooms. The guests were deeply offended by his rudeness. St Dunstan, partly for the careless boy's own sake, followed and made him return. It is even said that he dragged him back to his duties with his own hands.

You can imagine the rage of Edwig and his wife. It was so furious, encouraged by jealous courtiers, that St Dunstan was driven from power, all his noble work undone, and he himself obliged to leave the country.

The fall of the young king quickly followed. War broke out, and the kingdom was divided into two parties. Edwig was thrust from the throne, and his brother Edgar chosen by the Northumbrians and Mercians to take his place. Their next act was to send for the one man who could restore peace.

St Dunstan came back in triumph. The bishops of London and Winchester placed themselves and their people in his hands for the service of the king, and in less than two years the whole of Wessex had submitted.

SAINT DUNSTAN

It is said that eight vassal-kings rowed King Edgar in his boat on the River Dee, for Dunstan had made him lord over them all.

Edgar loved and trusted his great minister, for he had the wit to see that the famous churchman was the best man in the kingdom. He was made Archbishop of Canterbury, and held his own for sixteen years.

Sixteen years of peace! That was very wonderful in those old, rough days. And they were not idle years. Many wise laws were made by St Dunstan. At times he was a stern ruler, but his aims were always noble, and the king was his true friend. 'Edgar's law', as it was fondly called in after years, was the work of Edgar's great minister.

He founded new abbeys and schools. He invited the most learnèd scholars of Gaul to Wessex. He helped traders. Best of all, slavery began to disappear by the will of the Church.

I must tell you a few of the old ways of setting a slave free. They are well worth remembering.

Sometimes the slave's owner gave him up at the altar of the Church. Sometimes they would go together to four crossroads, then his lord would bid him travel wherever he wished. But the best way of all was for his master to take him by the hand, before a crowd of people, point to the open door and the open road beyond it, and give him the sword and lance of a freeman.

The life of St Dunstan, crowded with cares, brought out the full vigour of his nature. He never wasted an hour of the day. Of all his work, his heart was chiefly given to the reforms, or alterations, he thought would be good for the bishops and priests of the Church. In this matter he was strict, cool, courageous, doing as he pleased, obliging all the other men in high places to obey him.

At the death of Edgar, the king for whom he had ruled so long, there were violent quarrels over the choice of the next king. St Dunstan acted with his usual spirit. He crowned Edward, his old friend's son, and won the consent of the Wise Assemblies, as the meetings of nobles and churchmen were called, by forceful persuasion.

But the good years were over. The young Edward was slain by his enemies among the West Saxons and another king set upon the throne.

St Dunstan retired to Canterbury, shocked and stricken with sorrow. We know he did not seek to be revenged, for he afterwards crowned the new king. But his public life was over. He was getting old.

There is a beautiful proof of his unchanged love of music. He heard in a dream the whole of a sweet melody or chant. On awaking he wrote down the notes, and himself taught the boys of his choir to sing it.

St Dunstan was fond of all children. Once, when he was away from home, he saw a vision of a little boy he knew being carried away from the earth by a band of angels. When he returned, and a monk ran out to meet him, the archbishop cried:

'Are you all well here?'

'All well, my lord', was the quick reply.

'*All?*' he repeated.

'No – I forgot', began the monk; 'there is one who has been called to his heavenly home....'

'I know who it is. I know it is the little boy' – and St Dunstan told him his name and the hour of his death – 'I saw him in a vision in the hands of angels'.

St Dunstan's pupils were very dear to him in the quiet last years of his life. He liked them to sit in his room, study, or talk to him freely without shyness. They little knew that the gentle, grave, quiet man had ruled a country, driven its foes over the sea, mastered its kings and made its laws.

It is said that when St Dunstan preached his last sermon, although he was ill and weary, his voice suddenly grew strong, his eyes were raised as if he saw a heavenly vision, and his face 'seemed to dart forth rays of light'.

Two days after, on Sunday morning, he passed away at the hour of sunrise. St Dunstan was buried in

Canterbury Cathedral.

One last word.

I hope you all know that the home that was started during the Great War for blinded soldiers, where they are helped and trained to return to their old lives, is called St Dunstan's. Is it not well that the brave men, to whom we owe the deepest gratitude of our hearts, should be welcomed and cared for in a house that bears the name of a great English saint?

ST HUGH OF LINCOLN

SAINT HUGH OF LINCOLN

Twelfth Century
Festival ✦ November 17th

Our own Hugo of Lincoln is to my mind the most beautiful sacerdotal figure known to me in history.... Hugo's power was in his own personal courage and justice only; and his sanctity is clear, frank, and playful as the waves of his own Chartreuse well.
— John Ruskin

Let us look back, once more, into the days of old. The bright yellow broom of the Plantagenets was the royal flower of England, at the time I write of, for Henry the Second was on the throne.

He reigned for thirty-five years. Many great men were his friends or foes – St Thomas à Becket was perhaps the most famous but there is one figure that stands out from them all. Why, do you ask me?

Because it is the figure of a saint, one of the wisest, most holy, and bravest servants of our Lord; because he was gentle and true; because the poor blessed and the cruel feared him; because he loved this country as dearly as his own; because he loved freedom; because he loved a good jest; because he loved children and they loved him; because he worked and loved work.

Boys, he was called the Hammer of Kings, and in all your favourite stories of soldiers or great adventurers, you will not find any man to admire for his bravery and strength more than this great Englishman.

His name was St Hugh of Lincoln.

I have just called him an Englishman, and I will not take it back, although St Hugh was born in France. But he lived in England so many years, and he was so like the Englishman at his best, that I am sure we can say he belonged to our people.

He was Bishop of Lincoln. There is an old statue in the cathedral supposed to be meant for him, and scenes from his life are painted in the stained glass of a rose window, but they are not at all clear.

The grand cathedral itself is a monument for him, changed as it is since he built that noble church, but we cannot look upon its towers without remembering St Hugh of Lincoln.

The first Bishop of Lincoln was a Norman monk, and most of the men who followed him were courtiers, or held their posts by the favour of kings. Our saint was very different. Neither court nor king could turn him aside from his duty.

'I fear no mortal man', he once said.

That was the strange thing about him. He was so

bold – and so humble. He knew the ways of the busy world, but it never changed his nature. At the end of his long life, he was still the devoted Carthusian monk of early days, the servant of God and His Church.

St Hugh of Lincoln was the child of a noble French soldier, named William of Avalon. His mother, the Lady of Avalon, was very good and fair. He had two brothers, the elder named after their father, William, the younger called Peter.

Little Hugonete, as one of his schoolmasters called him – 'Hughie' we should say in English – sang sweetly as a boy and was dearly beloved by them all.

His father, almost from the child's babyhood, meant him to become a priest. I am afraid this fact made for great strictness. When he wished to join in the games of other boys – 'No, Hugh', he would hear on all sides; 'thou art to give thy life to holy things. Thou must not waste an hour of it'.

The death of their dear mother, when Hugh was about seven, made a vast difference to the three children. The Lord of Avalon had already left the army. He put the management of his estate into good hands, and found a guardian for his elder boys. He meant to spend the rest of his life at a priory, or religious house, at Villard-Benoît, near the town of Grenoble.

So thither he rode with his youngest son. He

dismounted when they drew near to the place, took the little Hugh by the hand, and led him to his new home.

You can imagine how the small French boy, shyly pressing close to his father's side, stared with his dark eyes at the sombre building and quiet, grave gentlemen who received them. I think they must have treated him very kindly, for he grew very fond of the priory, but not to stay in it, as his father did, for all time.

At fifteen Hugh was ready to take his vows. He wished to be a monk, but four years passed before it was allowed. He often wondered what his duties would be when he was no longer treated like a schoolboy.

To his great joy, the good prior, head of the house, ordered him to attend on the Lord of Avalon, who was getting old and weak. Hugh had always loved his father, and nothing could have given him greater happiness than to wait upon him, read to him, and slowly pace the priory grounds with the old soldier's arm drawn through his.

So the first quiet years of his religious life slipped away. It was a life that gave him time to study, pray, and attend faithfully to all his duties as one of the youngest brothers in the priory.

But other thoughts were gathering in his mind. The great wish of his life was taking form.

There was a monastery – it stands on the same spot today – called the *Grande Chartreuse,* where an order of monks, founded by a saint named Bruno, lived in a desolate, wild part of the country. Their rules were most severe. They had given up all pleasures. They lived in narrow cells, ate the plainest food possible, drank only water, slept little, rarely spoke to one another, did penance for their sins, tried to think only of Heaven, and prayed continually for mercy.

St Hugh was a Carthusian – these monks were called Carthusians – at heart, but at first they refused to allow him to join their order. They feared it would be too strict, and that he was still too young to know his own mind.

So he waited patiently for a while, until after his father's death, and it is even said that he promised one of his old masters at the priory at Villard-Benoît not to go to the *Grande Chartreuse*. If it were so, he was unable to keep the promise, for a day came when he fled from the priory to the Carthusian monastery and begged them to take him in.

The refusal was not repeated.

St Hugh lived with the Carthusians in solitude, poverty, silence, and obedience for ten long years.

Now, as I told you at the beginning of this chapter, Henry the Second was king of England.

Henry was a strong-willed, keen, fiery man of violent temper, 'orderly in business, talkative, impatient, never resting, with some charm of manner, but rough and obstinate; a fair scholar, a great hunter'.

In short, as far from a saint as it was possible for a man to be.

There was a Carthusian monastery at Witham in Somersetshire. It was a failure for the need of a good ruler. Henry was anxious to restore this monastery, but he could think of no English churchman fit for the difficult post.

Then, by good chance, he met a French count well informed in such matters, who told him of a certain Hugh of Avalon, who had been made procurator – or manager of affairs – at the *Grande Chartreuse*. The Frenchman described Hugh fully, and the king, who was quick in thought and action, sent a noble band, headed by the Bishop of Bath, to ask the head of the Carthusian Order in France to send St Hugh to England to become the prior of Witham.

A few days before the Englishmen arrived at the *Grande Chartreuse* with their king's letter, St Hugh dreamed that his own old prior, Dom Basil, appeared before him. Dom Basil had recently passed away, to the monks' great sorrow. He cheered St Hugh, told him of a coming change, and bade him be fearless.

In spite of his belief in the truth of this vision, St Hugh at first refused to leave the *Grande Chartreuse*, doubting his own powers. But the English bishop begged him to consent, and his own superiors bade him go.

I think it must have been a great pang when this man – modest, unused to the world – left his little peaceful cell and all his friends behind and started with strangers for a strange land. He did not know a word of English – he never spoke it well – and he knew nothing of the difficult, passionate, blunt king who had sent for him.

You must remember that kings in those days held the lives of their subjects in their hands. St Thomas à Becket had been killed by four of Henry's knights, and very likely there was not a man in his kingdom who thought that any monk in the world – least of all a humble Carthusian monk from overseas – would dare oppose him after that.

They little knew the Hammer of Kings!

It was not long before Carthusian Hugh had made his own discoveries about Henry, and Henry about Hugh. Both the monastery and church at Witham were in ruins, and the first work of the new prior was to rebuild. The king promised to help him, with many words of encouragement and kindness, but when the time came he refused to pay the workmen.

The prior refused, in his turn, to be left in the lurch. It was a first trial of strength, carried on without ill-feeling on St Hugh's part and with good temper, not unmixed with surprise, on the part of the king.

The prior won, not only the victory in this first dispute, but the respect of his opponent.

Strange as it is, when we know the selfish, violent nature of Henry, there was something in him of the true and great that was stirred and kept alive by St Hugh. It was a feeling that grew in spite of everything and made them friends. I think our saint, hammer as he did at Henry's faults and falsehoods, liked and forgave the rough man in his heart, for Hugh never bore malice, never hated, and saw the spark of heavenly goodness that God has hidden in the hearts of all men, even the lowest and the worst.

It is said that King Henry, on one of his voyages between Normandy and England, was nearly shipwrecked. He prayed for safety, crying aloud:

'O Lord! for the sake of my Carthusian Hugh, spare me!'

The ship lived through the tempest, and the king honoured his Carthusian Hugh more than ever.

Although the prior of Witham managed everything in the monastery, he lived as simply as when he was at the *Grande Chartreuse,* strictly obeying the rules of the order. Nothing was farther from his thoughts than the great honour which was thrust upon him.

After the death of the Bishop of Lincoln no effort had been made to choose another, for both the king and the clergy were inclined to let the matter drift. At last, when they gathered together to settle it, you will not be surprised to hear that the well-known prior of Witham, who had rebuilt his church and monastery, was the man whom they all wanted. The king gave his consent. Then, and not till then, St Hugh was told.

It was the old story of King Henry's first offer over again. He refused to go to Lincoln, as he had refused to go to Witham. His English friends could not move him. So they wrote to the head of the *Grande Chartreuse*, who commanded St Hugh to accept the bishopric. He gave way at once, for every Carthusian is bound to obey the superiors of the order.

The day came for leaving Witham.

A great company of nobles, soldiers, clerks, and priests were to ride with St Hugh towards London, where the ceremony that would make him a bishop was to take place at Westminster.

It was a grand and glittering show. The nobles were richly dressed and their horses decked with gay colours and bright harness; the soldiers' weapons shone in the sunshine; the priests wore their finest robes.

In the midst of all this splendour, ambling along on his mule with its old leather saddle, rode the new bishop, in the rough habit of the Carthusian monk, with a bundle of sheepskins, on which he always slept, strapped behind him.

I doubt whether he noticed the difference between himself and the others; he had always ridden so, and why should he change his ways? The same sun shines upon the poor man's ragged cloak and the rich man's jewels, he would have said, and the same green carpet of springing grass is beneath the silk shoe and the bare foot. The same blue Heaven is above us all.

After a little while one of St Hugh's followers managed to cut the cord that held the bundle of sheepskins, for he could not bear to see the courtiers smiling at his beloved master, and it fell to the ground and was lost, while St Hugh rode on, happily thinking it was still behind him.

After the ceremony at Westminster, which made the simple Carthusian a lord of the Church, he set out at once for Lincoln. He was at least five days in reaching the end of the long journey. The people came out to meet him, anxiously wondering whether their new bishop would prove to be as good a lord over them as they hoped by the stories they had heard of him.

He dismounted and walked to his cathedral – the cathedral so long neglected that it was half in ruins – and the men, women, and children pressed round him, trying to read his face. Would he help and protect them? Would he be kind and merciful? Would he love them as a father, or crush them as a cruel tyrant? Would he be generous to the poor?

That very night the last question was answered. The chief forester of the bishopric came to ask him how many deer should be slain for the feast to be given in honour of his coming.

'Three hundred, or as many more as are needed', replied the new bishop.

'Three hundred, my lord!' cried the man, in surprise; 'three hundred deer for your one feast!'

'No, for many feasts', said the bishop calmly; 'I want all the people of Lincoln to feast with me, but in their own homes. Take the deer, I beg you, and divide the best venison freely among the poor'.

It was done, and St Hugh was perhaps the only man who supped, when the day of the feast came, on dry bread. Although he now and then drank a little wine, he ate the hard fare of the Carthusian Order all his life.

Now, I will tell you why this generous gift of the bishop meant so much to the people of Lincoln.

There were many deer forests in the country at that time, for hunting was the chief sport of the king and his court, but the poor were not allowed to join in the chase or share the spoils. The land, that should have been as free as the air for the use of all, was stolen away, and the foresters, or servants who looked after the deer, were as harsh and greedy as their lords. The common people were treated as if they were wild animals, robbed by these proud, heartless men, half starved, and obliged to do their bidding like slaves.

In St Hugh the poor found, directly as he became bishop, a warm friend. His great heart ached for their suffering, but he did not waste a day in useless sighing. He warned the foresters that all the power of the Church would be used if necessary against them.

The worst tyrant of all, chief forester of the country, was a hard, powerful man named Galfrid. He was hated and feared, even at court among the people who pretended to be his friends.

His first meeting with the new Bishop of Lincoln was in the hall adjoining King Henry's private room. No doubt he thought the monk-like bishop, who was known to be humble and quiet, would be afraid of him when they came face to face.

'How now!' exclaimed the forester, in a loud, rude voice, making every one listen; 'what art thou doing here, close to the king's chamber? Canst thou not stay in thy church?'

'What art thou doing here?' replied St Hugh. 'Begone to thy forest!'

This quick speech was like the thrust of a dagger, for it showed the royal forester he had met his match.

It was not the only time, as you will hear directly, that St Hugh's ready tongue served him in good stead.

The courtiers ran to the king and repeated what they

had heard. Henry was very angry, for Galfrid was one of his favourites. He waited for a chance to vent his ill-humour on the bold bishop. It came quickly. At the death of the Canon of Lincoln, soon afterwards, Henry sent a message to St Hugh asking for one of his own friends to be given the vacant post.

'No!' replied St Hugh; 'the canon of a cathedral should be a churchman, not a courtier. I refuse'.

He did not even write, but told the messenger to repeat his words to the king.

I need hardly tell you that this firm refusal made the king more angry still. He sent for the bishop to visit him.

Henry went into the forest, when he heard St Hugh was coming, and forbade his attendants to show any mark of respect or return his greeting. He himself sat down, and did not trouble to raise his head or speak a word. When St Hugh came near he bowed, with his usual courtesy, but not a man in the crowd of courtiers dared to welcome him.

Then St Hugh sat down beside the king, quite calmly, but Henry took no notice of him. Nobody spoke or moved for several minutes.

Perhaps the king found it confusing, or he may have wished to provoke the bishop by a petty slight. At all events, he bade a servant bring him a needle and thread, and began to sew a little piece of linen round one of his fingers that he had cut by accident with a knife.

'Now', said St Hugh, smiling and speaking very quietly, 'you remind me of your ancestors at Falaise!'

Henry gave a big start, glanced in his face, tried to look very fierce, and then burst out laughing.

Now this was the point of the joke. Henry the Second was the great-grandson of William the Conqueror, and William's mother had belonged to the common people, for she was a poor working girl of the town of Falaise in Normandy, well known for its tanyards.

'My lords! My lords!' cried King Henry, in the middle of his laughter, 'this bishop has dared to tell me that I look like a poor glovemaker of Falaise'.

After that they talked of the choice of the canon for the cathedral, and Henry saw that St Hugh was right.

The proud forester, Galfrid, was sternly punished by St Hugh for his cruelty to the people of Lincoln, but in after years he became the bishop's loyal friend. That is very wonderful to think of. It shows us the power of our saint, who hated wrong, but loved and forgave the wrongdoer.

The cathedral at Lincoln was in ruins, as I told you, when St Hugh became bishop. He made up his mind to restore and rebuild it.

This was a great work – a glorious offering of man's love and reverence to God, for all the people joined in it, rich and poor, priests and monks, labourers and artists.

St Hugh himself worked among the men, carrying bricks and mortar and hewing stones, giving all the time he could spare from other duties. It is said that a miracle took place during one of his hours of labour.

A poor crippled man was bearing a load of stones upon his bent shoulders. He felt tired and walked slowly. Suddenly a hand was laid on his arm.

'Let me bear the stones for thee, my son', said a voice that he thought belonged to one of his fellow-workmen.

The load was lifted from his shoulders, and, at the same minute, he was filled with strength and vigour. He drew himself up to his full height. Behold! his twisted limbs and bent back were as straight as a boy's; the pain and weariness of many years was gone; he was a cripple no longer.

It was St Hugh who had carried away the heavy stones, and when the man rushed after him and would have kissed his hands and feet, pouring out his story, our saint very gently stopped him:

'Be silent, my son, and praise God!'

You must not think that St Hugh's busy life in the world made him neglect reading and study. He founded a school to teach religion, besides adopting several boys, who were educated at his expense.

I have already told you that he had always cared for

children. Even quite small babies left off crying when he came near, stretching out their arms with smiles and little fond sounds. Alone with a child, the bishop was a happy man – gay, playful, tender.

He was never sad or gloomy. One of his friends wrote that he was 'full of mirth, confident, and witty', and he said of his own quick tongue, 'Pepper is not more biting than I am, but I do believe there is not one' (he meant among his priests) 'who distrusts my love for him, nor one by whom I do not believe myself to be beloved'.

It was the truth. If they feared him a little – for he would sometimes give a man a cuff as well as a sharp word – they always loved him. He was ready to listen to advice and sought it humbly from others. He had begged the Archbishop of Canterbury, on first going to Lincoln, 'to help him to do his duty'.

He expected much from his own priests, not learning, perhaps, or fine sermons, but charity and faith and obedience.

'God will not ask of any man to have been a monk or a hermit', he said, 'but to have been truly a Christian'.

St Hugh rarely talked of miracles, or cared to hear about them.

'I need no greater miracle than the holiness of the saints', was another of his sayings.

Whenever it was possible to return to his first home

in England, the monastery he had built at Witham, he went there to live the life of a Carthusian, if only for a few weeks. He would put aside the robes of a bishop, the only difference between himself and the other monks being his bishop's ring, and spend the days and nights praying, thinking deeply, and in doing humble tasks for the brothers.

The building of the great cathedral went on, although it was not finished during the lifetime of St Hugh.

Whenever King Henry, who often went a-hunting in Selwood Forest near Lincoln, tried to raise money by seizing on any property belonging to the bishopric, he found 'his Carthusian Hugh' as brave as of old in opposing him. In this he strengthened English liberty, for it was a time in history when kings were altogether too powerful and the common rights of the people little heeded.

Henry was angry again as of old, but knew him too well to use force. Lincoln's bishop became famous all over the country for his courage and fair play.

Now, before I tell you what happened to our saint after the death of King Henry, I am sure you would like to hear the story of his swan. It is one of the best of the bird stories, and there are many good ones, ever told.

In nearly all the pictures of St Hugh there is a big

swan painted at his feet. It has become his emblem. Foolish people have sometimes laughed at the legend, not believing it to be true. There is no good reason why we should doubt it.

There are people in the world today, and always have been, who love and understand all living creatures so well that the most timid, and also the fiercest, animals make friends with them. If you are not afraid – if you are really so kind that you would not give pain to one of these 'brothers and sisters' of ours, as another dear saint has called them – you will be able to win the affection of the shy bird, the sensitive horse, the faithful dog, even the wild, fearless things that we only find in open fields and mountains and forests.

A mighty hunter is often a great man; but, believe me, there is a greater man still – a mighty lover of God's living works.

The hunted deer, the dead lark, the crushed butterfly – what are they? Spoilt! Dull! Ugly! But the living deer is a marvel of strength and beauty; the living lark fills the sky with music; the living butterfly is like a flower with wings – the fairest jewel that flashes in the sunlight.

About eight miles from Lincoln there was a place called Stowe. A short time before St Hugh paid his first visit there the people had noticed a strange bird on the lake.

It was a big swan, with snowy feathers and a bill tinged with yellow. It drove away the other swans, after choosing one of them to be its mate, and was so wild and shy that no human being, standing on the shore, had a chance to see it closely.

Directly as the bishop approached the lake, the amazing bird flapped the water with its wings, giving a loud, hoarse cry, came on shore, and followed him like a dog right into the house.

It ate from the bishop's hand, stood beside him while he slept, and thrust its head up his wide sleeve, nestling against his arm.

This did not happen once, but again and again. The people said that they knew when the bishop was coming, because the swan flapped the water and flew ashore to be ready to meet him.

The last time that St Hugh went to Stowe it is said that the swan was very sad. It stayed in the lake, with drooping head, silent. Did it know that its kind master would never be there again? I cannot tell you. I only know that the story of its love for our saint was told by several of his friends and companions, who saw with their own eyes what I have described to you.

Long, long before he went to Stowe, St Hugh had tamed little birds and squirrels that came into his cell at the *Grande Chartreuse,* and shared his daily bread with them.

When Henry the Second died, his son, Richard the Lion-hearted, became King of England.

As violent, but less crafty than his father, Richard was a brave soldier and a strong king. St Hugh was no longer a young man, but his first message to the new king, after he had been crowned at Westminster, shows the old, undaunted, bright spirit.

He was on his way to Richard's feast, with friends and attendants, when he saw the body of a dead man lying at the edge of the road. The man had been killed by robbers, or a wicked enemy.

The bishop stopped, and gave orders for the burial. As he was about to begin the prayers for the dead, one of Richard's knights came galloping along the road and drew rein beside him.

'The royal feast is ready, my lord', he cried; 'the king is waiting for the Bishop of Lincoln'.

'For Heaven's sake let him begin his feast', said St Hugh; 'tell him I am busy in the service of the King of kings'.

The knight rode away again, but he gave the message in a trembling voice. All the courtiers knew the hot temper and pride of Richard. But they misjudged him for once. He listened quietly and nodded, leaning back in his chair.

'We will wait for the Bishop of Lincoln', he said.

It was not the first time St Hugh had so attended

SAINT HUGH OF LINCOLN

the burial of a stranger. It was a frequent custom, in those days, to ask a priest to do his holy office at the roadside. Children were often brought to him by the peasants to christen, as he rode about the country. He never refused, however busy, to bury the dead with solemn rites, or baptise the people's children, or say prayers for the sick.

Sufferers from leprosy, which is a very terrible illness, moved him to many acts of charity. He went to see them, prayed with them, helped them in every way he could think of to bear their trouble. St Hugh stooped, one day, and kissed a leper on the cheek, whispering holy words of comfort in his ear.

'My lord bishop', said an attendant standing by, 'it is said that St Martin cured a leper by his kiss of peace. This man is unchanged by thine'.

'It is true that the blessèd St Martin cured the body of a leper by his touch', was the grave reply; 'and this poor brother hath cured the ills of my soul by his'.

On the return to England of King Richard from the Crusades, he tried to raise money, as his father had done before him, by seizing on Church property, but the Bishop of Lincoln once more resisted. The king's officers were afraid to use force, and even the Lionheart himself gave way at last to the Hammer of Kings.

At the end of Richard's reign of nine years, his

brother John came to the throne. The false and wicked John pretended to look upon St Hugh with kindness. They met abroad, and the bishop gave the new king good counsel.

Our saint had never seen the home of his youth since he was first called to England. You can imagine his feelings of fond remembrance as he drew near to Avalon, where he met once more his dear brothers, William and Peter; to Villard-Benoît, where his father had taken him as a little boy to the quiet priory; most of all, as he turned his face towards that desolate spot in the mountains where he had loved and served God when he was young.

It was a beautiful summer day on which Carthusian Hugh, dismounting at the hill which was too steep for his horse, walked to the end of his journey, and looked once more with tears in his eyes at the walls of the *Grande Chartreuse*.

His heart was too full for words at the brothers' tender greeting. For three weeks he stayed with them, at rest and peace after his long, hard fight with the world, then he lifted the burden once more and bade them a last farewell.

His name had travelled before him. Crowds of people, the great and learnèd, the poor and humble, flocked out to see the Bishop of Lincoln as he passed through France. It was the same when he landed at Dover.

Old friends were there to meet him, new friends to beg his blessing. People brought their children that they might look upon him. The Archbishop of Canterbury asked him at once to go to London, and thither he hurried, although he was very tired and ill.

He went to his London home in the Old Temple. His health, long failing, broke down at the end of the journey. He began to sink rapidly. His ardent life had been like a fire, burning steadily on, with many leaping flames; but at the end it glowed more faintly every day.

He knew that he was dying, and thanked God that his heavenly rest was drawing near. He made his will, when his friends urged him, leaving all he had to be given to the poor.

When the end was near, he asked for some ashes to be dropped upon the ground in the shape of the Cross. Then he was lifted from his bed and laid upon it. He folded his hands in prayer, over the rough hair shirt that he had always worn as a Carthusian monk, and his great heart ceased to beat. His soul passed away to his Maker.

All London mourned. The body of St Hugh was taken back in honour to his own Lincoln.

Slowly, solemnly, with lighted candles borne before it, the funeral procession passed through the country. There were throngs of people all the way to see it go by. It is said that many miracles took place. There was the sound of weeping everywhere.

King John of England and King William of Scotland were waiting for the procession at the great cathedral in Lincoln, surrounded by the people whom the noble bishop had served so bravely and loved so tenderly.

Let us honour the name of St Hugh of Lincoln by remembering his message to Christians, of his own and all future times:

'Charity in the heart, truth on the lips, and purity of life'.

SAINT ZITA

Thirteenth Century
Festival ⚘ April 27th

O Light of lights, Redeemer of mankind,
Whose glory most in mercy shines displayed,
Concede Thy favour to my humble mind,
Increase my feeble memory with Thine aid,
My heart today some fitting words would find,
To tell of Zita, Lucca's holy maid:
That Christians all may read her life, and how
She sleeps in old San Frediano now.
       – Ballad of Santa Zita

THIS is a little, simple story of a little, simple saint. Although she lived to be an old lady – sixty years is a long time to look forward to when you are young – she did not change very much.

She was not a princess, like St Etheldreda; or an empress, like St Helena; or a friend of great men, like St Catherine of Siena; or a leader of armies, like St Joan of Arc.

She did not choose to be poor to escape the idleness of wealth, as so many saints have chosen poverty, because she was poor already. She did not only work for the good of her soul, but because she had to earn her daily bread.

In brief, she was a little servant. Now, let me tell you all about her.

In that part of Italy that is called Tuscany there is a town named Lucca. It is on a river, and there are beautiful mountains to be seen in the distance.

It was a busy, cheerful place when St Zita lived there. That was in the thirteenth century – twelve hundred years after our Lord. Her home was not in the city itself, but in a village close by.

There were a great many silk merchants in Lucca. Many of the people were very rich. The houses were finely built; useful, pretty clothes were worn; children went to good schools; the churches were adorned with fair pictures and sculpture. There had been bishops of Lucca for over six hundred years.

There was one church older and more interesting than the others. It was called the Church of San Frediano. I shall have a tale to tell you about it later on.

St Zita's mother was a poor woman. She had several children, but I think Zita must have been the eldest, for she helped her mother to keep their tiny house in order.

Think of the difference between the life of this little Italian girl and your own – if you live in a good house, with books to read, pretty frocks to wear, presents on your birthday, holidays in the summer, and no end of pleasant occupations and amusements.

Zita had none of these things. She had to clean the floors, wash the vegetables, spin, dig in the garden, run on errands, and take care of the other children. But you need not pity her at this time of her life. She was treated kindly by her mother, and the neighbours were very fond of her. They all found her such a quiet, good-tempered, gentle little creature.

The days are very sunny in Italy. When Zita rose in the early morning, slipping softly out of bed so as not to disturb her little brothers and sisters, she looked up into the clearest blue skies in the world.

Such lovely skies! They made her think of the bright angels of Heaven and the noble army of martyrs with palm branches in their hands. Her mother had told her about them, and she thought of the olden days when our Lord lived among men, and called little children to Him, and she wondered whether He would have come to their village and noticed such a tiny place as her mother's house.

That thought made her eager to begin the day's work and make every corner of the tiny house clean and sweet to be ready for Him – if He came again. Zita's mother had given her two rules as a guide in whatever she did.

'This is pleasing to God, I must do it', was the first.

'This would displease Him, I must not do it', was the second.

She tried to keep the rules every day. It was easy at home, for her mother was always near to help her, but the time came when it was very hard indeed to obey them.

Zita was obliged to earn a little money, as they were so poor, directly as she was old enough to go out to service.

Her mother talked to the neighbours. They all agreed that it would be best to send her to some house where other servants were kept, for they would teach the child her duties and take care of her. The friendly village people judged others by themselves. They had known Zita all her short life, and would have laughed at the idea of anybody treating her unkindly.

'She is such a good, obedient girl', they said; 'all her fellow servants will be pleased with her'.

So a 'place' was found for the poor woman's daughter in the house of a family named Fantinelli. Her few clothes were put together; she kissed her mother, brothers, and sisters – they were all in tears at the parting – and went off by herself to serve strangers in a strange house.

How old do you think Zita was? Perhaps sixteen? Oh, no! Four years younger than that. She was only twelve.

There were both men and women servants in the Fantinelli household.

The master was a hot-tempered, impatient man, of whom they were all afraid. The mistress was more good-natured, but rather a lazy, careless person. The children were left in the care of nurses, for neither of the parents paid them much attention.

No one seemed to expect Zita. No one spoke a word of welcome. The lady of the house had forgotten all about engaging her. Some of the children, meeting her on the stairs, stared and laughed at her bare feet and poor clothes.

She was given a tiny garret to sleep in. Her duties were to wait upon the other servants.

All the girls in the house were older than Zita. They copied the idle, vain habits of their mistress, did as little work as they possibly could, and grumbled at that. The men, in their turn, behaved as much like their master as they dared.

Fantinelli was a rich man, but in debt to half the tradesmen in the city. The chief servant, to whom he trusted his money for the expenses of the house, was both wasteful and dishonest in trifles.

Poor little Zita! At first she was too shy, and too confused by the number of people in the big house, to speak a word to anybody. She kept her garret very clean, did everything she was told to do as well as she could, and tried to keep out of the way.

Her master, the first time he asked her to do something for him, shouted so roughly that it made her tremble, and she nearly burst into tears. Her mistress was surprised, and a little amused, by her quick obedience.

Her fellow servants were angry with her for doing her work so well. It began to make them ashamed of themselves, and that is a very unpleasant feeling. They said she was a little fool, and one of them, more cruel than all, struck her with such force that she fell down and was badly hurt. The others only laughed.

The poor child crept up the steep stairs to her garret. She was faint and ill from the blow.

She knelt down beside her hard bed and began to pray, as her mother had taught her to do when she was in trouble. Her eyes were blinded with tears.

She thought of her little brothers and sisters and the kind village people. No one cared for her – and she had tried so hard to please them – in this big, noisy, grand house. They did not give her enough food, they mocked at her way of speaking, they did not even let her go to church, except to early Mass, before it was time to get up.

Now, although Zita cried so bitterly, she was not angry with anybody in the house. She felt that it *must* be her own fault that they treated her so unkindly. She was too humble a little creature to blame them.

Then she thought of the sufferings of our Saviour; her own were nothing compared with His. It consoled her greatly. She began to think of herself as a servant of God, not of Fantinelli, and she made up her mind to work as if the place belonged to Him and He were her only Master.

There was a change in the household from that day, but it came very, very slowly.

The men and girls were still unkind, but they looked at her now and then with half sullen, half jealous wonder. She was so sweet-tempered, so obedient, so obliging. They could hardly believe that it was sincere.

Her mistress, to whom she scarcely dared to speak at all, heard her singing to the children one day, when Zita thought they were alone, in a voice as soft as the cooing of a dove.

Fantinelli himself, without being able to give any reason, spoke more quietly than of old and even tried to check his fits of passion when she was near. There was a look in her clear eyes that he could not understand. It did not seem to reproach him, but it made him feel sorry. His children, who had always shrunk away, began to treat him more fondly, and that gave him a strange feeling of tenderness he had never known before.

Zita's work became harder as she grew up. The other

servants knew they could depend upon her help. She often did their work as well as her own. It was 'Zita, do this!' or 'Zita, do that!' all day long.

She had so little time in her garret, for she laboured from sunrise to sunset, that she learned to pray and think of God in the midst of her toils. Her mind and heart were filled with heavenly thoughts while her hands were busy with daily tasks.

There was only one sorrow in Zita's life. She had nothing to give away. Every penny of her small wages went to her mother, and she longed to be able to help the poor and suffering who begged in vain at Fantinelli's door.

The waste of money and good food, through the carelessness of her companions, troubled Zita very much, but it was not her place to speak of it. Fantinelli was a generous man if he had a purse in his hand, but he was too lazy and self-satisfied to seek out the poor or care about them. No one thought the little maid wanted to give alms. She never asked for any present, so they never thought of giving her one.

The servants found out that Zita knew how to make good bread. As they liked it to be baked just in time for breakfast, she was obliged to get up very early. But this was no hardship, for she had made it a rule, as I told you, to go to church while the others were still sleeping.

One morning, after Mass, Zita was so deeply happy in her beautiful thoughts of our Saviour that she forgot all about the passing of time. She was in the Church of San Frediano – if ever you go to Lucca you are sure to see it – where she knelt in silent prayer, filled with rapture and thoughts of heavenly delight.

She had forgotten her work, her home, her friends. She felt like the blessèd apostles when they looked upon Jesus Himself in His divine beauty and love.

The church was empty. A ray of sunlight fell across the ground, where Zita knelt, like a halo all round her. She looked like a saint indeed, with her shining, upturned face, her trembling, clasped hands. It was the sublime hour of her life.

A cloud passed over the sun. There was a peal of bells from a neighbouring church.

Zita sprang to her feet, as if she had been startled out of heavy sleep. The remembrance of her neglected duties rushed over her. She did not stop another minute.

She ran through the streets to Fantinelli's house, her cloak fluttering in the wind, her little roughshod feet pattering on the stones.

It was nearly breakfast time and the bread would not be ready! She had never been so unhappy or ashamed, but, at the same time, her heart was still throbbing with the bliss of her thoughts in church.

She opened the door and hurried into the kitchen. There, on the table, stood the bread, carefully kneaded, and quite ready to put into the oven.

As Zita stood still, panting, she became aware of the perfume of flowers in the air – were they roses or lilies? – but there were none to be seen. The sweet scent filled the room. It seemed to float round her like a summer breeze, lifting her hair and cooling her face.

Zita went upstairs, directly she had put the bread in the oven, to beg her mistress's pardon for being so late and thank her for doing the work. She felt sure that the lady herself had prepared the dough, it was so very well done. But her mistress knew nothing about it. None of the servants had been down to the kitchen that morning.

It was very strange. They were all puzzled. When the time came to take the bread out of the oven they crowded round, eager to see the mysterious loaves.

Little Zita lifted them carefully on to the table. The crust was golden-brown, the crumb was snowy white, and once again the smell of freshly gathered flowers floated in the air.

The lady of the house looked into her little maid's face, while the servants chattered and questioned, and then she went to find her children. They ran after her willingly down to the kitchen. The youngest of all, whom she carried in her arms, laughed joyfully and stretched out its little hands when it caught sight of Zita.

'I want you to take care of the children in future, Zita', said the lady.

Zita stooped, kissed her hand and thanked her humbly. She was very grateful.

Then the lady went to her husband and spoke to him in secret.

'This is a blessèd day for our house', she said; 'for an angel from Heaven has crossed the threshold'.

Fantinelli stared at her. He saw she was very pale and her eyes were full of tears.

'Say you so?' he cried, half in doubt, half in mockery; 'what wonderful things hath the angel done?'

'Made the bread for our little servant!' replied the lady.

Many years passed by.

Zita still looked upon herself as the lowest servant in the house of Fantinelli, but her master and mistress had placed their household affairs in her hands. It came by degrees, beginning with trifles.

At first the other servants were jealous, but as she still did her own work, and waited upon them as of old, their jealousy did not last long. They began to like her – love her – listen for her soft voice, admire her quiet face, wait for the sound of her willing feet.

Zita was afraid of good fortune, more afraid than she had ever been of hardships. She prayed unceasingly to God to save her from the sin of pride, and refused to leave her garret for a better room, or lessen any of her old labours.

She was able, by care and thought, to pay Fantinelli's debts out of the money he gave her to keep the house. She even managed, by thrift, to save a goodly sum for her master.

'Spend it for me, Zita', he said; 'it is yours to give in alms, or to keep as you will'.

This made Zita very happy. At last she had her wish. She gave every penny to the poor, in Fantinelli's name.

Zita rarely left the house, except to go to church, but many people went to see her, more and more as time passed. It is said that one hundred and fifty miracles were wrought, by the grace of God, through her piety.

Forty-eight years she lived in service. A bright star, on the night when her holy spirit passed away from earth, hung over the little garret where she lay. The people saw it through their tears. They never forgot her – they never will.

Her tomb is in the Church of San Frediano. She is the patron saint of domestic servants, and of the city of Lucca.

'Blessèd are the poor in spirit: for theirs is the Kingdom of Heaven'.

SAINT FRANCIS OF ASSISI

Thirteenth Century
Festival ✦ October 4th

He is wise who imitateth the wise man; he is good who imitateth the good man ... he is noble who imitateth Him who is noble, namely, our Lord Jesus Christ.
— Golden Sayings of Brother Giles

HAVE you ever heard of 'the poor little man of God'? That is the name St Francis of Assisi gave to himself.

I do not think, of all the followers and friends and servants of our Saviour, of all those who most truly loved and understood His words, there was ever a man more simple, great, gentle, and brave than Francis.

He is the most lovable of all the saints in many ways, and the most Christlike. You will hear how true he was as a friend, how dear to him were all living things, and how he won the hearts of his fellow-men.

Even today, seven hundred years after his time, people love to read about him. His adventures are all well known. His name shines out, in our list of saints, like a star that is more beautiful and bright than all the other stars.

Assisi, where St Francis lived, is in Italy. His father was a rich cloth merchant named Bernardone.

In those days it was the custom for merchants to travel, buying and selling their goods, to different cities. Bernardone even went as far as France, and during his absence in that country his little son was born.

The mother had him baptised by the name of John. But when the father returned home he called the baby Francis, or 'the little Frenchman', and Francis he remained ever afterwards.

He was a happy child, not too carefully educated, though he learned a little Latin, but could only write with difficulty. He used to dictate his letters, in later years, signing them with a cross. His chief pleasure was in listening to his father's descriptions of his travels, with news of religion (all the people were interested in Church affairs) and wars in foreign lands.

His mother was a gentle, quiet woman. When the neighbours talked of the gaiety and thoughtlessness of her boy – for the young Francis was inclined to be wild and reckless – she calmly replied:

'Do not be hard upon him. I am very sure that, if it please God, he will become a good Christian'.

He was indeed a lively youth, spending his father's money in all sorts of quaint and foolish ways. His friends were the richest young men of Assisi. He excelled them all in gay attire, and the love of merry jests, pranks, feasting and song. But with all his absurdities, Francis was refined and courteous.

He went into his father's business, too, being as apt in making money as in throwing it away, but his wild companions often called him from his work. The merchant did not complain, for he liked his son to be seen with rich and high-born friends. It was only when Francis, who never could refuse a beggar, emptied his pockets and even stripped off his handsome clothes to give to a poor man, that Bernardone was angry.

He forgave the boy's careless extravagance, but he could not understand his frank charity. But then he never understood his son, for Francis was so different from himself.

Francis was a poet and a knight. His high spirit made him seek for adventures. When a war for the freedom of the people broke out in Assisi, Francis, although he was only seventeen, joined the ranks, fought bravely, but was taken prisoner.

He surprised his fellow captives by his good humour and gaiety. He hoped for a glorious future in those days, talking about it to anybody who would listen.

'You will see', he would say merrily, 'that one day I shall be adored by the whole world'.

He little thought his words would come true, but in a way he never dreamed.

The prisoners, after a year's confinement, were set free, for the war was over.

Francis returned to his father's house at Assisi. The old life began all over again – feasting, singing, dressing, wasting money on light and empty pleasures. But his health broke down, and he was ill for a long time.

A winter passed in dreary days. The poor boy crept out of the house when there was the first feeling of spring in the air.

He slowly made his way, leaning on a stick, to the nearest city gates, passed through them, and looked out upon one of the fairest and most peaceful scenes in Italy.

As his weary eyes wandered over the open plains, with the hills in the far distance, decked in the beautiful colours of the cedar, the oak, the vine, and the olive, a feeling of remorse crept over him. He thought of his idle youth, for the first time with regret. His old restlessness came back, but he felt that the old pleasures would no longer satisfy him.

The sadness and longing for a different life became so great that he suffered a pain more sharp than even in the worst hours of his illness.

His happiness and gaiety were gone for the time being, but he tried to bring them back on regaining health and strength by joining a gallant knight of Assisi in a journey to a distant part of the country, where a little war was being waged.

Francis bought himself so handsome an outfit that all his friends in the city were talking about it. If he had been the son of an earl, instead of a cloth merchant, he could not have spent more money or awakened greater envy. But what do you think he did the day before starting? Gave away all his finest clothing to a poor knight who was in need of it.

When Francis left Assisi he seemed to have regained his high spirits.

'I know that I shall become a great prince', he said.

So he bade his family a gay farewell, mounted his horse, and rode away with the little troop to win fame and fortune.

In a very short time, almost before the excitement of the leave-taking was over, Francis had returned to Assisi – alone, broken, and silent.

Perhaps his comrades had treated him cruelly because of his boyish boasting; perhaps he could not endure their rough company; perhaps he had already heard the voice of our Lord calling him to a very different life.

At all events, a change had come over him. He began to take long rambles about the country, with a friend who proved his affection by never seeking to pry into his thoughts. He often went alone to a grotto, among olive trees, where he prayed for help, for his old dreams of pleasure and fame had passed away. He no longer wished to be a prince, or to be adored by the world.

At last his young friends, after failing to win him back as a boon companion, invited him to a special feast and made him the king of the revels.

Francis seemed to join them with his old mirth, but when they were going home together at the end of the feast, shouting and singing, he was suddenly missed from their company.

They turned back and found him, still holding his sceptre as king of the revels, but so lost in thought that he had forgotten all about them.

'What is the matter with Francis?' they laughed.

'We know! He is thinking of the fair one he loves. He is going to take a wife!'

'True!' cried Francis, with so strange a smile that he looked a different man; 'I am thinking of giving my love to a lady more beautiful and good than you can even imagine!'

That night marked the turning-point in his life. He never again joined in revels of the old kind. He passed longer and longer times in solitude, but he was too strong a man to waste himself in vain regrets.

The poor farmers and labourers on the land round the city of Assisi were often very poor, because of the wars, illness, and bad harvests.

They began to find a friend in Francis, who helped them not only with money but with true sympathy. He understood their troubles as if they had happened to himself. They felt that he too had suffered.

It was very strange. This son of a rich merchant, this jester and singer of gay songs, was able to fill them with hope and courage.

He was so grateful for their affection that he began to ask himself the question – how does it feel to be really poor? Why are the poor, of all people, so generous and free in giving to others? Why did our Saviour care for the poor so much? Would it be possible to endure hardships and give his whole life to others?

At last, while these ideas were growing in his mind, Francis exchanged clothes with a beggar and stood a whole day, fasting, outside a church, with his hand held forth for alms. It hurt his pride, but it moved him to pity he had never felt before. It made him think, with all the passion of his deep, simple nature, of our Saviour's appeal, and he seemed to hear the divine voice speaking to him: 'Follow thou Me'.

It was not easy, for Francis was too earnest to follow Christ as so many are content to follow Him. He longed to serve Him utterly, to prove his loyalty and love, but it was two years before he gained the victory over his own worldly desires.

On a certain day, as he was riding by himself,

thinking of his Lord and King, a man who was suffering from leprosy begged for alms.

Leprosy is a dreadful illness. It is dangerous even to touch one who is suffering from it, and Francis felt a shock of horror. He wheeled his horse in another direction, but a minute afterwards he felt the shame of a coward. He called himself a knight of Christ and he had disobeyed his Leader!

He turned again with bitter self-reproach, leapt from the saddle, and ran to the poor creature on the road. He gave him all his money, and then, lifting his wasted hand, pressed it warmly to his lips.

This was a victory for Christ. His soldier had not failed him.

A few days afterwards Francis went to the place where the lepers were made to dwell all by themselves. Try to imagine how they felt when a handsome young man, in the flush of youth and health, came amongst them in their misery and tended their sores, with tears of heavenly pity in his eyes, words of heavenly comfort on his lips, tenderness and kindness – no shrinking away – in the very touch of his hand.

Francis no longer felt any horror, and his heart overflowed with love and joy when he read the gratitude in their wondering eyes.

Have you forgotten that Francis told his companions,

on the last night when they feasted together, that he hoped to win a lady more beautiful and good than they could even imagine?

Now, they thought that he meant a real, living girl whom he wished to marry. It was not so. He was speaking of poverty – his Lady Poverty – and he spoke in that way because he was a poet. At that time many rich, proud men pretended to be humble Christians. St Francis did not dispute with them. He simply made up his mind to be poor, as Jesus was poor.

There were few who understood him. His father was angry because he cared no longer to work in the business or be seen with important friends.

The Bishop of Assisi, from whom he sought advice, thought he was a foolish dreamer. Doors were closed against him. The people believed he was going mad.

I have not time or space, in this short chapter, to tell you of the long, hard struggle before St Francis became a free man – free to follow his Lord and free to love his Lady Poverty.

He left his home, gave up his horse, his money, and his clothes. He made himself a rough grey habit to wear. He was chased through the streets of Assisi and pelted with stones and mud. The old cloth merchant, after trying to break his spirit with violent ill-treatment, turned him out of the house.

He was all alone in the world, living on the broken

food of a beggar. But he was happy. His soul was filled with gratitude. He loved God's beautiful earth, and his love of God was like a burning fire in his heart.

His first work was to rebuild, with his own hands, a little ruined chapel called St Damian's. Then he returned to the poor lepers, and lived among them in brotherly kindness.

His high spirits had returned. He sang songs as of old. He would do any work that came to his hand, but without payment. Instead of wine, he drank of the clear, pure water of the running brooks. Instead of meat, he ate the bread of loving charity.

Then he began to preach – first of all in the streets of his own city of Assisi – and the hearts of men were moved to new faith. They saw our Lord through his eyes, for St Francis was the 'mirror of perfection'. They called him madman no longer. He set an example, in his poverty and devotion, that one after another of his friends began to imitate.

Francis had prayed for a few companions to help him in his work. Never was a prayer more fully answered.

The first of that little band of brothers – the first and the dearest of all – was named Bernardo. St Francis opened the Gospels, when Bernardo first went to him, and read:

'Go, sell whatsoever thou hast, and give to the poor, and thou shalt have treasure in heaven; and come, follow me'.

So Bernardo, who was a rich youth, gave away all he possessed, with Francis standing beside him in the marketplace of Assisi, and they were joined later on by the young Brother Pietro, the devoted Brother Leo, the gentle Brother Giles, the childlike Brother John, the ardent Brother Juniper – and many, many others. The wisest men and the most simple obeyed him.

So began, following the pure example of the poet and knight of Assisi, the great Order of the Friars Minor. If ever men trod in the footsteps of Jesus Christ – loving, serving, trusting, living in poverty by hard work, and preaching the truths of God – those men were St Francis and his first brothers.

They helped the labourers in the fields; they were not ashamed to beg; they returned good for evil; they were cheerful, and kind, and friendly.

Of all the churches where they prayed, the brothers loved best the small church called St Mary of the Portiuncula. The last word means 'little portion', a name that was very dear to our saint, who loved to think of it as a blessèd spot that God had given to them.

It is there that roses grow without thorns, and St Francis said of it:

'This place is holy. Let the holiest friars of my order live here'.

You see this wonderful man became a father to

those who joined him. As he was the most humble, greatest, unselfish, and inspired of them all, so he was also the most beloved.

The Friars Minor went up and down the country, sleeping in hay lofts, leper hospitals, or in church porches. They were never sad. They worked with delight, and the people began to give them welcome wherever they went. There were still some who thought they were mad, you may be sure, for it was hard for men and women to understand the happiness of these strange beings – without money, roughly clothed, often despised and mocked.

When the brothers were sometimes troubled at the few who really desired to imitate Christ, St Francis told them of his visions of the future:

'I see a multitude of men coming towards us, to receive the habit of our holy order.... Lo! the sound of their footsteps echoes in my ears'.

His words came to pass. Not dozens, not hundreds, but thousands of brothers joined the Friars Minor during the lifetime of St Francis. Thousands have belonged to it ever since.

Now, the time came when the love of St Francis for God and his fellow-beings widened into a love for all things in the world.

The birds, the beasts, the fishes, became his little

brothers and sisters. The sun, the rocks, and the water were equally dear to him. How could he dare to pray to God if he did not love the creatures of His making?

St Francis would turn aside not to tread upon a worm. He preached to the birds in these words:

'Brother birds, you ought to praise and love your Creator very much. He has given you feathers for clothing, wings for flying, and all that is needful for you. He permits you to live in the pure air; you have neither to sow nor to reap, and yet He takes care of you, watches over you and guides you'.

After this sermon, St Francis's friends tell us, the birds began to arch their necks, spread their wings and open their bills, as if to thank him. Then he went in their midst, for they showed no fear of him, and stroked them.

On another day, when St Francis was about to preach to the people, the swallows so filled the air with their chirping that he could not make himself heard. So he silenced them by crying:

'It is my turn to speak, little sister swallows, listen to the Word of God. Keep silent and be very quiet until I have finished'.

St Francis loved the flowers too, and when they were sowing vegetables and other useful plants at the Portiuncula he told the Friars to keep a corner for 'our sisters the flowers of the fields'. Their perfume was a joy to him. 'In touching them, or looking thereon', says Brother Leo, 'his spirit did seem to be not upon earth but in Heaven'.

One day, when our saint was crossing a river, the boatman made him a present of a big fish he had caught that was still alive. Francis thanked him and accepted it gladly. Then, to the man's surprise, dropped it again into the water and bade it swim home with his blessing.

The prettiest story is of a tiny insect called a cicada. It has a very loud note for its size.

When a cicada perched on his finger, chirruping its little heart out, St Francis smiled with delight, and after a time raised his voice softly and sang with her.

Now, you shall hear the good tale of the wolf of Gubbio, in the words of one of the brothers of St Francis:

'In the days when St Francis abode in the city of Gubbio, a huge wolf, terrible and fierce, appeared in the neighbourhood, and not only devoured animals but men also; in such wise that all the citizens went in great fear of their lives, because ofttimes the wolf came close to the city. And when they went abroad, all men armed themselves as they were going forth to battle; and even so none who chanced on the wolf alone could defend himself; and at last it came to such a pass that for fear of this wolf no man durst leave the city walls.

'Wherefore St Francis had great compassion for the men of that city, and purposed to issue forth against the wolf, albeit the citizens, with one accord, counselled him not to go. But he, making the Sign of the Cross and putting all his trust in God, set forth from the city with his companions; but they fearing to go farther, St Francis went his way alone towards the place where the wolf was. And lo! the said wolf, in the sight of much folk that had come to behold the miracle, leapt towards St Francis with gaping jaws; and St Francis, drawing nigh, made to him the Sign of most Holy Cross and called him, speaking thus, "Come hither, brother wolf; I command thee in the name of Christ that thou do no hurt neither to me nor to any man."

'Marvellous to tell, no sooner had St Francis made the Sign of the Cross than the terrible wolf closed his jaws and stayed his course; no sooner was the command uttered than he came, gentle as a lamb, and laid himself at the feet of St Francis. Then St Francis speaks to him thus, "Brother wolf, thou workest much evil in these parts, and hast wrought grievous ill, destroying and slaying God's creatures without His leave; and not only hast thou slain the beasts of the field, but thou hast dared to destroy and slay men made in the image of God; wherefore thou art worthy of the gallows as a most wicked thief and murderer: all folk cry out and murmur against thee, and all this city is at enmity with thee. But, brother wolf, fain would I make peace with them and thee, so that thou injure them no more; and they shall forgive thee all thy past offences, and neither man nor dog shall pursue thee more."

'Now when St Francis had spoken these words, the wolf, moving his body and his tail and his ears, and bowing his head, made signs that he accepted what had been said, and would abide thereby. Then said St Francis, "Brother wolf, since it pleaseth thee to make and observe this peace, I promise to obtain for thee, so long as thou livest, a continual sustenance from the men of this city, so that thou shalt no more suffer hunger, for well I ween that thou hast wrought all this evil to satisfy thy hunger. But after I have won this favour for thee, brother wolf, I desire that thou promise me to do hurt neither to man nor beast. Dost thou promise me this?" And the wolf bowed his head and gave clear token that he promised these things. And St Francis said, "Brother wolf, I desire that thou pledge thy faith to me to keep this promise, that I may have full trust in thee." And when St Francis held forth his hand to receive this pledge, the wolf lifted up his right paw and gently laid it in the hand of St Francis, giving him thereby such token of good faith as he could. Then said St Francis, "Brother wolf, I command thee in the name of Jesus Christ to come with me; fear nought, and we will go and confirm this peace in the name of God." And the wolf, obedient, set forth by his side even as a pet lamb; wherefore, when the men of the city beheld this, they marvelled greatly....

'And the said wolf lived two years in Gubbio, and was wont to enter like a tame creature into the houses from door to door, doing hurt to no one, and none doing hurt to him. And he was kindly fed by the people; and as he went about the city never a dog barked at him. At last, after two years, brother wolf died of old age; whereat the citizens grieved much, for when they beheld him going thus tamely about the city, they remembered better the virtues and holiness of St Francis'.

If there were more room and time I could tell you many other stories of St Francis.

You will often hear the name of St Clare when people talk about him. I cannot now tell you the whole story of this holy maiden. But she called herself 'a little plant of poverty in the garden of St Francis'.

·He founded an order for women, very like the Order of Friars Minor, and a young girl of eighteen was the first sister. This was St Clare. She understood his rare nature, held him in reverence, and followed our Lord as faithfully and wholeheartedly as he did.

St Francis did not live to be an old man, for he was worn away by hardship and suffering. Thousands had joined the Friars Minor, as I told you, but none of those who came after him equalled the founder.

Once, at a great meeting of the brothers, he suddenly

came among them – some of them thought that he was far away, some of them thought he was no longer alive – and the mere sight of him moved them to tears of rapture, cries of welcome, prayers and blessings.

He died as he had lived, full of love and tenderness and joy.

He was in Assisi when the end was drawing near, surrounded by some of the brothers who had joined him first – Brother Leo, Brother Angelo, and others. He begged to be carried to his dear church of the Portiuncula, where he had lived in the wonderful days of his youth. So they lifted him in his bed and bore him thither.

When they reached a part of the road between the church and the city he asked them to set him down. His eyes were failing. He was nearly blind, but he turned his face towards the home of his childhood and solemnly blessed Assisi.

When they told him that death was very near, he bade the brothers sing in love and praise of God, and he 'spread out his hands towards the Lord', and with much cheerfulness of mind and body said: 'Welcome, my sister Death!'

Would you like to know the song that our dearest saint wrote and loved to repeat – the song that his brothers sang to him before his soul passed away?

It is called the 'Canticle of the Sun'. The word canticle means a song or chant. It is rather long, but I hope you will read it carefully. Remember that it came from the joyful, loving heart of the blessèd Francis:

> Most high, omnipotent, good Lord,
> Praise, glory, and benediction, all are Thine.
> To Thee alone do they belong, Most High,
> And there is no man fit to mention Thee.
> Praise be to Thee, my Lord, with all Thy creatures,
> Especially to my worshipful brother sun,
> The which lights up the day, and through him dost
>   Thou brightness give;
> And beautiful is he and radiant with splendour
>   great;
> Of Thee, Most High, signification gives.
> Praised be my Lord, for sister moon and for the
>   stars,
> In Heaven Thou hast formed them clear and precious and fair.
> Praised be my Lord for brother wind,
> And for the air and clouds and fair and every kind
>   of weather,
> By the which Thou givest to Thy creatures
>   nourishment.
> Praised be my Lord for sister water,

The which is greatly helpful and humble and precious and pure.
Praised be my Lord for brother fire,
By the which Thou lightest up the dark,
And fair is he and gay and mighty and strong.
Praised be my Lord for our sister, mother earth,
The which sustains and keeps us
And brings forth divers fruits with grass and flowers bright.
Praised be my Lord for those who for Thy love forgive,
And weakness bear and tribulation.
Blessèd those who shall in peace endure,
For by Thee, Most High, shall they be crowned.
Praised be my Lord for our sister, the bodily death,
From the which no living man can flee.
Woe to them who die in mortal sin,
Blessèd those who shall find themselves in Thy most holy will,
For the second death shall do them no ill.
Praise ye and bless ye my Lord and give Him thanks,
And be subject unto Him with great humility.

SAINT CATHERINE OF SIENA

Fourteenth Century
Festival ⚊ April 30th

Blessèd are the clean of heart: for they shall see God.
— St Matthew 5:8

YOU will find the life of St Catherine of Siena, as I hope to tell it to you, different from the other chapters in this book.

We will begin at the beginning, but we will not go on to the end. I mean, you shall be told all about a wonderful child, but it will be better if you wait a little, until you are old enough to read the history for yourselves, before you hear of her grown-up days.

She did not live to be very old, for she died at thirty-three, but her life and work as a woman had to do with so many people – popes, friars, grand ladies, poor prisoners, princes, rulers – that you would find it hard to follow.

There is not any saint better known or more beloved. Over forty books have been written about her. Some day you may read her own letters.

She was an angel of love and pity. Her faith was

so simple, but so deep in her secret heart, that many people cannot begin to understand it. All her thoughts were so good and holy that only to look upon her face, or listen to her voice, made the proud humble, the sick well, the wicked sorry for their ill deeds.

It is nearly six hundred years since St Catherine lived, but she seems to step out of the past, when we begin to think of her, like a bright spirit from the hand of God.

Siena is the name of a town in Italy. It is a City Beautiful, built on the top of a hill, with domes and towers and roofs clustering within its old walls. The streets are narrow and steep.

The people who lived there during St Catherine's girlhood are thus described: 'Men and women in coarse clothes; many wore plain leather, and the women were without ornaments. Their manners were simple, and in many ways they were rude and blunt, but they were of good faith and loyal. They were a warlike people, restless, never feeble, full of energy'.

In a winding alley, or passage way that could hardly be called a street, lived Catherine's father, a dyer named Giacomo Benincasa. His wife was called Lapa. They had a big family of children, twenty-five in all.

Giacomo was a mild, sweet-tempered man. If he heard angry words passing between his boys and girls he would say:

'Now, now, do not speak any words that are not just and kind, and God will give you His blessing'.

All the neighbours liked him. He was not only true and honest in big things, but in everyday speech. No rude or bad word was ever heard in his house.

Lapa's father – our little St Catherine's grandfather – had been a poet. Lapa was very fond of all her children, and taught them to be truthful and patient.

Catherine had a twin sister, Jane, but she died as a baby – 'winged her way to Heaven'.

Catherine was little more than a baby herself when she began to toddle to the neighbours' houses, for she was very friendly and not at all fearful. They were all fond of her. She talked prettily and was so good-tempered and loving that they gave her the pet name – rather a hard pet name to remember! – of Euphrosyne. It is a name that means 'joy'.

I must tell you that she was given many names, or titles, in after life. Would you like to hear them, although they may seem strange to you? She was called the Daughter of the People, the Beloved Sienese, the People's Catherine, and the Gracious Lady of Siena.

When Catherine was only six years old she saw the first vision of her life.

She was sent, with her little brother, Stephen, to

take a message from their mother to a married sister who lived at some distance from their home.

The two children were returning by the valley when the sun was setting. It was a lovely evening, calm and still.

The light of the fiery clouds fell on the end of a church that Catherine knew well. As she glanced up at it, shading her eyes with her little hand, it seemed to her that the sky opened and she saw the figure of our Saviour, shining in golden robes, glorious to behold.

She stood still. The people who were passing by, little knew that her wondering eyes were raised to Heaven in fear and happiness too great for words. They only saw the clouds of sunset, flame colour and purple.

Our Saviour bent His head and looked at Catherine. He smiled upon her. She forgot everything – the road beneath her feet, the sounds in the air, the voice of Stephen calling to her.

If she had had wings like a bird she would have flown into the light and nestled at His feet. As it was, her little heart was filled with joy and love and gratitude.

When her brother came running back, unable to make her hear him, she burst into tears, for as he touched her hand the vision faded.

'O Stephen! if thou couldst only see what I have seen thou wouldst never have called me on'. She cried all the way home, looking up at the sky as it grew dark and darker.

From that day onwards, her friends thought, the little Catherine grew more thoughtful and grave.

Catherine, when she was a few years older, began to think of copying the Fathers of the Desert. These were holy men who lived in wild and lonely parts of the country, in caves or little huts they built themselves, to pray and think of God by day and night.

At first she did not dare to go far from home, for the little girl felt very shy when she found herself among strange faces in streets where she had never walked alone.

Then she grew more bold. One morning, very early, she slipped out of her little bed, dressed, took half a loaf of bread, and started out in earnest 'for the desert'.

Now, 'the desert' was a long, long way off, but Catherine did not know anything about that. When she had left the city behind her – for the first time in her life – she thought that her journey must be nearly over. The houses were at some distance from one another, there were no shops, and the country looked very lonely and lovely in the quiet morning air.

At last she saw a small grotto, or cave, half hidden under a piece of rock.

She crept in – sweet little hermit with her soft eyes

and shining hair! – and knelt upon the ground to pray.

All day she stayed there. If there were any passers-by they could not see her. She ate all her bread, believing that Heaven would give her food on the next day.

She was very happy, thinking of her vision of our Lord. The grotto was cool and shady even at midday. Now and again the shadow of a bird flitted past, or she heard the whisper of the wind in the trees.

In the life of St Catherine, written by one of the friends who knew her best, we are told that towards the end of the day 'God showed her that she was meant for another kind of life from that of a hermit, and that she must not leave the house of her father'.

In other words, it would have been very wrong for the little girl, as her own heart told her, to keep away from home for more than a few hours. Think how anxious her poor father and mother would have felt! We can never please God by making others unhappy.

So the child came out of her hiding-place and ran home as fast as she could, not afraid of her parents' anger, but so sorry for their anxiety.

St Catherine was not a beautiful girl. We have all met people who are not beautiful, but whom we admire with all our hearts.

Her face was long and delicate, with grey – some of her friends tell us hazel – eyes; her chin and jaw were rather too big. Her smile was gay and winning. She moved with grace and talked quickly. She was frank and cheerful, looking at any one with whom she spoke kindly, but very keenly. She bowed low to strangers, and even knelt down to receive the aged, or truly religious men and women.

Her parents, when first she wished to become a nun, sent for a reverend priest to talk to her. They thought it was only girlish folly. The good man did not know what to think of her. She spoke so gravely, but she looked such a child.

'My daughter', he said at last, 'if you really mean to give yourself to God's service, prove it to us by cutting off your hair, for none of the holy maidens you wish to join are vain, as you may be'.

St Catherine's long hair was golden-brown and glistened in the sunshine. She cut it off, quickly and eagerly, smiling at the good priest. It was strange, she thought, that he should ask her to do so small a thing! But her parents would not let her go after all.

Once St Catherine dreamed that she was changed to a man, and had become a monk of the Order of St Dominic. It was a grief to wake up and find herself still a girl. She used to gather other girls about her, lead the way to a quiet spot, and preach to them 'with wonderful power'. If they smiled at her, they loved her none the less.

Some of these children imitated her manner of living when they grew up, and remained her friends and fellow-workers for life.

It was the custom at that time for girls to be betrothed when they were very young. Catherine's parents and elder brothers were anxious to arrange a marriage for her. Her father thought it would be well for his daughter to be the bride of a young man who had proposed for her and seemed, in every way, to be suitable for her husband.

Catherine, gently but firmly, refused the youth's repeated offers. She was sorry to disobey her parents – it was the first time she had ever done so – but she had made up her mind not to marry. They thought it was a mere fancy, for they did not know how earnestly she had prayed, or how deeply she had thought over the matter, before deciding.

It was not easy for Catherine, for her family tried to break her will. They loved her and wished her to be happy, but they did not see that she was really different from other girls. We must not blame them too much, or think they meant to be so unkind, but there is no doubt she suffered very much from their severity.

Catherine gave up her own little room, at their bidding, although her greatest joy was to be there alone, pouring out her heart to God.

She did the hard work of the house willingly and

well. Indeed, she became a little drudge. At times she longed to give way, for the thought of marrying and having a home of her own was very sweet, but her love of Christ was so great that it drew her back to Him again and again. It was as if she had heard Him say – as His first friends, the apostles, heard Him say – 'Follow Me!'

This silent struggle between Catherine and her parents went on for a long time. Her brothers often said to one another, 'We are beaten. Catherine has won!' but her father could not see it. He mistook her meekness for obstinacy.

As she had to share a room with a little brother, Catherine was not able to pray aloud or sit in silence, thinking of holy things as she used to do in happier days. But it taught her a good lesson. It taught her to think of God in busy hours, to withdraw her thoughts – do you know what I mean? – from the talk or noise going on round her and fix them on the mercy, or the strength, or the loving-kindness of her Saviour. Perhaps you will not understand all her meaning, but this is what she says:

'I built in my soul a private closet, with strong walls of the Divine Providence, and kept myself always close and retired there. By this means I could find peace and repose in my soul, which no trouble could interrupt or disturb'.

One of her dreams at this time was of the appearance of St Dominic, the founder of the famous order of the Dominicans, who came up to her smiling, and said:

'Daughter, be of good cheer, for the day is coming when you shall wear the mantle you so much admire'.

Catherine, on awaking, believed that this meant that the wish of her heart would be granted, which was to put on the cloak, or mantle, of the Order of St Dominic. The dream came to pass in later years, and she wore the black and white habit of the 'Militia of Jesus Christ', founded by that famous saint.

This 'mantle' meant a great deal to Catherine, for it was the first step towards becoming a preacher. She loved all her fellow-creatures with so burning a love that she longed to save their souls by telling them of the true faith.

One day her father went into her room, unheard, and saw that she was praying.

He stood still, looking at his child in amazement. There was a clear, bright, soft light all round her. In the middle of it, over her bowed head, hovered a white dove.

Her father crept out of the room, covering his eyes with his hands.

He sent for Catherine soon afterwards and all the other members of the family.

Once more he asked her to consent to marry. She told him, in simple, fond words, that nothing could alter her. She could not marry. 'It would be easier to move a rock', she said, 'than to move me'. But she would be their servant gladly. If they turned her out of the house, He whom she served would protect her.

Her mother burst into tears. Even her brothers wept. She was so loving and gentle, but so firm. There was no sound in the room but the sound of their sobs. At last her father spoke.

'I knew what your final answer would be', he said; 'God keep us, my dearest child, from opposing you any longer. You have proved that the Holy Spirit commands you. You shall do as you please in future. Pray for us that we may be grateful to our Lord for joining you to Himself at so tender an age'.

Then Catherine humbly thanked her parents, and they all rejoiced together.

Her room was given back. She was no longer treated with any unkindness.

For three years she hardly left her little room, but lived to listen to the voice of God deep in her own heart. She ate very sparingly, and slept on bare planks without any covering. Her garments were spotlessly clean and neat. She was always cheerful and kind.

Catherine loved to think that prayers were perpetually rising to Heaven from the people's part of the city, where her father's house stood, so she did not sleep at night, but lifted her voice in prayer till the church bells sounded for the first morning Mass. Then, and not till then, she lay down to rest.

Those were hard and often painful days, for her health was weak and she suffered much, but her courage and strong will never failed.

Great work in the world lay before Catherine. That pious girl, in her quiet room in the dyer's house in Siena, was known in after years as a noble soldier of the Church, a preacher who turned the hearts of men and women from evil, and won the love and reverence of Italy.

As I said at the beginning of her story, some day you must read for yourselves the full life of this extraordinary saint.

Now we will leave her in her little room, kneeling in the light of her faith, with the white dove from Heaven hovering over her head.

SAINT JOAN OF ARC

Fifteenth Century
Festival ⚜ May 30th

The things that I have spoken,
I heard them from God.
The light I saw was the true light.
— Girolamo Savonarola

I WILL tell you last the story of the warrior Maid of Orléans. It is one of the bravest stories in the world. It is the life of a dauntless soldier in the noble army of martyrs; and, at the same time, it is a tale of a simple country girl.

Joan of Arc could not read or write. She hardly knew her own age. She had never travelled or studied, or talked with wise men. She had been a timid child. She did not hope for power, or dream of winning it. She knew nothing of soldiers, except to fear them, but she led the armies of France to victory. Her name is written, in letters of gold, in the list of famous generals of the greatest battles in history.

St Joan was born in a little village called Domrémy,

on the borders of Lorraine and Champagne, in the fair land of France.

Her father was a labourer, or small farmer, named Jacques d'Arc; her mother bore the pretty name of Ysabelle.

There were big woods near their home, where the children were allowed to wander, if they did not go too far away. They made garlands of flowers and hung them on the boughs of old trees, looked for fairy rings in the grass, and sang their own little songs by the clear, bubbling streams.

There was a beech tree in particular which our saint used to deck with wreaths in honour of Our Lady of Domrémy, meaning the Holy Mother of Jesus. Old folks told her that fairies haunted the spot. She never saw them, but one of her brothers declared that they appeared to him.

Jeannette, or Jeanne as her child friends called her, was a quiet, very good, simple girl. She was fond of going to church, but the only prayers or hymns she knew her mother had taught her when she was a little child. She learned to spin and sew, worked in the house, but did not go to the fields very often with the sheep and other animals.

It was a very unhappy time for France.

The famous King Henry the Fifth of England, who had conquered the country, was just dead, but the

English were still in possession of the greater part and were under the command of Henry's brother, the Duke of Bedford. The French king had also died, leaving a son and heir, called the *Dauphin,* who was not strong or daring enough to free the land from its powerful enemies.

Even the little far-away village of Domrémy suffered from the terrible years of war. The people were often obliged to fly to the woods, while bands of robbers, or rough soldiers, burnt their houses and carried away their property.

It is not strange that Jacques d'Arc, his family, and all his friends were very, very sad – almost in despair – when they thought of the troubles of their poor country.

The scattered French armies were quite unable to hold their own against the English Duke of Bedford. There was poverty all over the land. Ten thousand English soldiers held the city of Orléans. A hundred thousand people died of illness and misery in Paris. The *Dauphin* was helpless. It seemed as if God had forgotten France. But no! He never forgets.

The hour was drawing near for His soldier to come forth, in divine strength, to save her country.

Jeanne was thirteen years old.

One day, in the summer time, she was alone in her father's garden. It is easy for us to make a picture of her in our minds – the dark-eyed, strong, young French girl, in her plain dress and square shoes, with the light falling on her figure through the full branches of the trees, like a bright rain of sunshine that rippled over the grass at her feet, sparkling and shining.

Suddenly – she heard a voice. It was clear and musical and seemed to come from her right side, towards the church. At the same time a strange, lovely light – different from the flickering sunlight – floated in the air from the same place.

She was very much frightened, but that did not last long. She never told the words that the voice spoke on that summer day when it first came to her, but soon afterwards she heard it again, and saw the light again, in the shadows of the wood.

She believed it was the voice of an angel, sent to her from God. It told her to be good, in simple words she could easily understand, and go often to church.

Then a time came when it spoke to her again and again, two or three times a week.

'Go into France!' it said; 'you must go into France. Go into France!'

Her home, as I told you, was on the borders of Lorraine, and Jeanne knew that the words meant she should leave the village of Domrémy to do something for France. Now, the strongest feeling of her life was sorrow for her country's wrongs. In her own words, often repeated, she 'had pity on the fair realm of France'.

'Go!' said the voice; 'raise the siege which is being

made before the city of Orléans'.

Jeanne replied that she was only a poor girl, who knew nothing of warfare. How could she ride and fight? Who would follow her? Who would listen to her? What could she do?

Then the voice cheered her and said she must speak first to a certain captain, telling her where to find him.

So she went to stay with her uncle for a few days, to be nearer to the place where the voice directed her. Then she asked her uncle to take her to the captain's house, and he did so. She had never seen the captain, but she knew him at once, thanks to her heavenly guide. He would not listen to her. The first and second time he bluntly refused even to see her. But when he spoke and looked at her, the third time, he was so moved and bewildered that he gave her a guard of men and sent her to the Duke of Lorraine.

The duke, who thought she was a witch, began to ask her questions about his health. She quietly told him she knew nothing of that, but said she would pray for his well-being. Then she went back to the captain, for the foolish duke had sadly disappointed her, and he gave her a sword, and she put on the clothes of a man and mounted a strong horse. The captain chose a good knight, a king's messenger, and four servants to ride with her, and made them promise to treat her with honour and courtesy.

So she bade him farewell. He could hardly believe that it was possible for a young girl to help the *Dauphin*, who had become the King of France, although he was not yet crowned.

'Go!' said the captain; 'go, and let come what may. I think thou art inspired by God'.

So Jeanne and her companions rode away.

The voice that she heard became very clear to her at this time, and she often saw visions of two fair saints, St Margaret and St Catherine. She also said that St Michael and holy angels came to her, but she could not tell other people what they were like.

'Some had wings', she once said; 'others were crowned'. She kissed the earth where they had stood. She relied upon God, and loved Him with all her heart.

The King of France was at a place named Chinon. He had almost given up hope, for he wept every day and did not dare to face his enemies.

It was two days before he would see the maid from Domrémy, who lodged in the town with her companions. Then he sent for her, and many wise men, bishops and doctors of learning, were told to question her. She told them that God had sent her to save France. After three weeks she was sent by them to one of the king's generals, the Count de Dunois. He had the courage to say, as the captain had said, that he believed she was inspired by God.

She was then clad in armour, and carried a white banner in her hand on which was a painting of our Lord holding a lily.

Jeanne did not tell the Count de Dunois that she had given a sign to the king of her heavenly power, but I am sure you would like to know what it was.

It happened at midday in the king's house. An angel came into the room, floating along the air, but as he drew near to the king his feet touched the ground. He bore a crown. It was of fine gold, so bright and rich that no words can describe it. The angel bade the king trust to Jeanne and he should be crowned at Rheims.

The maid went into battle carrying her banner. She never killed a man with her own hands, but she gave them 'stout buffets and blows'. She had become a fearless rider, for she would mount a horse so ill-tempered that no one else would go near it.

Sometimes she carried a little axe in her hand. One of her banners was painted all over with lilies, with a picture of the world in the middle and an angel on either side. The words upon it were: 'Jesus, Maria!' in honour of our Lord and His Blessèd Mother.

She was given the command of twelve thousand men, but before the fight for Orléans began she caused a letter to be written to the English. It was a wonderful letter. She offered to make peace, if they would give back to France what they had wrongfully taken, and depart as friends.

'I am sent here by God, the King of Heaven', she wrote; 'I will drive you all out of the whole of France ... if you will not believe the message of God and the maid, in whatsoever place we find you we will enter therein. You, Duke of Bedford – the maid prays you that you do not come to grievous hurt. Answer, if you wish to make peace in the city of Orléans'.

The English defied her. So the battle began.

The maid herself placed the first ladder against the chief fortress, and was wounded in the neck. But she went on, crying to the soldiers to follow.

Her white banner – painted by the order of her voices – led the way to victory. A great wave of courage swept over the French. They were quite outnumbered by the English, but nothing could hold them back.

In less than twenty-four hours the little French army marched into Orléans, with Jeanne at its head, to the gratitude and joy of the whole city.

The news of the maid's first crushing victory was carried far and wide.

The people would have treated her like a saint; they tried to kiss her hands or touch her garments as she rode along, but she would not listen to their praises.

The simple, modest girl of Domrémy was all unchanged. She looked upon her dead enemies with streaming tears. She bade the soldiers pray, not feast and drink, in honour of victory. She made them treat their prisoners kindly.

She lived among these rough men – some of them the roughest and worst of men – as if she were indeed an angel from Heaven. She was so good and pure that all the French, from generals to common soldiers, looked upon her as divine.

When the English gathered their forces together, after the retreat from Orléans, the maid rode on from city to city at the head of the army.

Before one of the battles a French duke, with other leaders, asked her what was to be done. As before, they were outnumbered by their foes.

'Have all of you good spurs?' she replied in a loud voice.

'What do you mean?' they cried in alarm. 'Are we then to turn our backs and ride away?'

'No!' she said; 'it is our enemies who will not defend themselves, but retreat so quickly that we must have good spurs to pursue them!'

And it came to pass as the maid had said. The English took to flight, leaving behind them many prisoners.

When Jeanne was troubled, or uncertain what to do, she left the company of the soldiers to pray alone. Then, after a little while, she always heard her voices, sweet and clear, as she had heard them in the garden of her home, far away.

'Daughter of God! Go on! Go on!' they said. 'We will be thy help. Go on!'

Then the King of France joined his conquering army, and they went forward to the town of Troyes, a stronghold of the enemy. The king called his generals round him. Several of them had tried in vain to pass the outer forts. There were many different plans. They talked together long and earnestly. Then the maid suddenly came among them.

'My noble king!' she cried; 'waste no more time, but order your people to besiege Troyes. When my banner touches the outer walls it will fall into our hands. In God's name, before three days are gone I will lead you into the town in victory'.

She put herself at the head of her own men, gave orders to all, and planned an attack so well – 'indeed better than the finest generals working together had done', as the Count de Dunois said that in less than the three days the king's cause was triumphant.

The glorious maid went to church daily in Troyes. She called the priests together, when she had said her prayers, and they all sang a hymn in honour of the Blessèd Mary, Mother of our Lord.

She set a good example to her soldiers in every way, for she behaved to all men very quietly and modestly, and never allowed an evil word to be spoken, or a wicked tale to be told, in her presence.

After the victory at Troyes the king, with Jeanne and all his friends, went on to Rheims, where the maid had promised he should be crowned.

As they rode into that beautiful city, she exclaimed:

'How happy I should be if, when my days are done, I might be buried here'.

'Jeanne', said an archbishop, 'in what place do you hope to die?'

She lifted her dark, deep eyes to Heaven.

'Where it shall please God'.

Then she sighed and rode on a while in silence.

'I would that it was the will of God for me to lay down my arms', she said, 'and return to serve my father and mother, and take care of the sheep, with my sisters and brothers'.

Then she looked fondly at a ring her parents had given her. She always wore it.

So the king went into Rheims, with the maid riding beside him, and was crowned there.

Everything happened as Jeanne had said it would. The whole army held her in honour, not only because she was a fearless leader, but because no man could see her and speak to her without feeling that he was in the presence of a most wonderful human being.

All the letters that were written by men and women

who knew her well, and promised to speak the truth, tell us the same tale – they believed she was inspired by God.

She showed divine mercy to her enemies, and the lives of hundreds of men lay in her hands. She was true to our Lord's commands in word and thought and deed.

The English fled before her. She was wounded for the second time in the trenches near Paris, but recovering quickly, led the army on from victory to victory.

'Forward – forward, in God's name!' was the battle-cry of the maid.

'Do not fear numbers. Do not hesitate to attack', she cried when the generals would have drawn back; 'God will help us. I am sure that it is He who guides us'.

She was always in the front ranks. Her banner, painted with the lilies of France, never fell in the dust.

'In all she did', writes one of her commanders, 'she was a very simple young girl, but for warlike things – such as bearing the lance, assembling an army, directing a battle – she was most skilful. Everyone wondered that she acted with as much wisdom and courage as a captain who had fought for twenty or thirty years'.

Alas! the day came when this great soldier, this pure and gentle maid, was taken prisoner.

I wish I could tell you that she escaped. I wish I could tell you that she went home, after saving her country, to that peaceful little village where every soul knew and loved her.

Alas! it was not to be. She, who had lived so brave a life, died the death of a martyr.

Some say she fell into the hands of her enemies owing to treachery, for her victories had caused great jealousy among the French commanders.

It is certain that the King of France could have rescued her, but to his shame – to the shame of all his generals – he allowed her to be sold to the English.

I am sorry to tell you that she was treated with great cruelty. Her captors were so hard-hearted, and afraid of her at the same time, that they could not see the wonder of her life.

They called her a heretic and pretended to give her a fair trial, but the chief judge was one of her most bitter foes, a base and brutal man named Pierre Cauchon, Bishop of Beauvais. He did everything in his power to confuse and frighten her; his clerks did not write down her answers to their questions truthfully; there were men put into the jail to spy upon her; they even insulted her with wicked words, and put her into iron fetters.

The peerless maid faced her stern judges with unfailing courage. Her simplicity and truth baffled and conquered them. Nothing could shake her pure faith in the heavenly voices she had heard.

Day after day, without a friend near her or a single word of human sympathy, she stood alone in Christian fortitude and innocence. Absurd and trifling charges were brought against her. The false and cunning Bishop of Beauvais would not listen to any one who spoke in her favour. Many witnesses were forced to tell lies, for fear of their own lives.

It is dreadful to think of any men in the world being so unjust and cowardly. May God have forgiven them!

It was a long trial. I expect you know how it ended. Jeanne was condemned to be burnt to death in the marketplace at Rouen.

Let us try to forget this shameful trial, for it was publicly declared to have been unjust and unlawful twenty-four years after Jeanne's death.

Let us only remember that the last word she spoke was the name of One who had suffered, as she suffered, from the cruelty and the ignorance of His foes.

A man had given her a little cross made of a piece of wood, as they bound her to the stake, and she held it before her eyes and they heard her cry 'Jesus!' again and again. The executioner trembled and wept. Even the friends of the wicked Beauvais could not bear it and rushed away. One of the canons of Rouen burst into tears.

'God grant my soul may go to the place where I believe this woman's to be!' he cried.

The truest word of all was spoken by an English soldier:

'All is lost for us!' he groaned; 'we have burnt a saint'.

Our book has come to an end. You have read of many noble Christians in these pages – their holiness, their faith, their courage, their charity.

The legend of a brave soldier, Christopher, was the first of our stories; the life of a brave soldier, Joan of Arc, is the last.

There is no greater figure in many ways, in the history of all nations, than the simple village girl of Domrémy.

By leading the armies of France to victory she saved her country and died for freedom. In her mercy she spared her worst enemies; in her gentleness she wept at a harsh word; in her courage she equalled the boldest captain in the field. No evil word ever passed her lips. She stopped the foolish people who would have worshipped her:

'In God's name, not mine, the soldiers fight, and He alone can give the victory!'

She, who was the commander-in-chief of the French army, lived very quietly with any pious woman she could find for a companion. All the clever and practised cunning of her false judges could not prove her guilty of a single wrong deed.

She always spoke the truth and loved virtue. The men who had done her to death were hated by the people of Rouen, who had seen her pray in their churches and knew of her utter goodness.

She was a hero in war, a saint in life, a martyr in death. As long as the 'fair realm of France' is a land of freedom, the world will remember and honour St Joan of Arc.

THE END

About The Cenacle Press at Silverstream Priory

An apostolate of the Benedictine monastery of Silverstream Priory in Ireland, the mission of The Cenacle Press can be summed up in four words: *Quis ostendit nobis bona* – who will show us good things (Psalm 4:6)? In an age of confusion, ugliness, and sin, our aim is to show something of the Highest Good to every reader who picks up our books. More specifically, we believe that the treasury of the centuries-old Benedictine tradition and the beauty of holiness which has characterized so many of its followers through the ages has something beneficial, worthwhile, and encouraging in it for every believer.

www.cenaclepress.com

Also Available:

Robert Hugh Benson
The Friendship of Christ

Robert Hugh Benson
Confessions of a Convert

Fr Willie Doyle, SJ
Pamphlets for the Faithful

Dom Pius de Hemptinne, OSB
A Benedictine Soul: Biography, Letters, and Spiritual Writings of Dom Pius de Hemptinne

Blessed Columba Marmion, OSB
Christ the Ideal of the Monk

Blessed Columba Marmion, OSB
Words of Life on the Margin of the Missal

St John Henry Newman (*ed.* Melinda Nielsen)
Festivals of Faith: Sermons for the Liturgical Year

Dom Hubert van Zeller, OSB
Approach to Prayer

Dom Hubert van Zeller, OSB
Sanctity in Other Words

Visit www.cenaclepress.com for our full catalogue.

www.ingramcontent.com/pod-product-compliance
Lightning Source LLC
Chambersburg PA
CBHW041307240426
43661CB00037B/1461/J